Western States Native America

William (Bill) C. McElroy

Copyright April 2023

ISBN 9798392026692

Preface:

Each year tens of thousands of travelers visit the American Southwest/Western states and California. They go to the primary tourists sites like the Grand Canyon, and they miss much of the history of the people that originally settled the west, the Native Americans.

There are dozens of Native American Tribes throughout the United States of America, and this touring booklet covers those that live or lived in the west and southwester US. Their lives and their past is on display for you to understand, learn from, and help as many are in need. Tourism and Casino gambling is all that some tribes have for income, and many have limited resources like electricity and water.

This tour guide booklet is designed to help them, and to help you have a delightful and informative vacation in 'Indian Country'.

Table of Contents:

Chapter # 01 – Introduction:

The author has lived in the American Southwest several times and currently resides in Tucson, Arizona. He has traveled to many Native American reservations and Native American ruins over the last decade. The author has a series of tour guide booklets that cover the western states, and in each are sections on Native America and its presence, be it today as an active reservation or yesteryear as a now abandoned archeological ruin.

Ruins are protected; many are now Local, State, or Federal parks, and many are on protected Native American lands. Many of the active reservations have their own police, courts, jails, and laws and thus you as an invited guest need to know the rules, which are included in this touring guide booklet.

NOTE: The majority of the text in this manual is identical to the subject matter text that is in the author's individual State touring booklets. This booklet is a consolidation of those texts.

Chapter # 02 – Alaska:

The following text and pictures are from the author's book.

Alaska Adventures,
a Touring Guide

The guide for campers, RV owners, hikers, sportsmen, flyers, and
tourist

By William (Bill) C. McElroy
Copyright 2019 McElroy, William (Bill) C.

Alaskan Islands

Several of the Alaskan Islands have a small population of Native
Americans that are ancestors of the centuries old original settlers.
These are not considered to be tourist islands, but if you desire to
visit and can arrange transport and accommodations, feel free to do
so. Just remember that you are a guest and have to obey their laws
and customs.

The Islands have several Native American peoples that include the
Unangax, Atka, Alutiiq, Pribilof, Sugpiaq, Tlingit, Haida, and
Athabascan.

Your visit to the islands may include the islands of Atka, Kodiak,
Umnak, St. Paul, Baranof, and Adak.

The people are friendly and the activities can include fishing,
boating, crabbing, bird watching, kayaking, hiking, and learning
about the Russian fur trapper history that helped settle the islands.

Consider visiting the villages of King Cove on Kodiak Island, False
Pass on Umnak, Sand Point on St. Paul, Sitka on Baranof, and Adak.

Be ready to enjoy the magnificent views of the beaches, mountains,
and wildlife. Kodiak is the prime destination for most travelers.

Chapter # 03 – Arizona:

The following text and pictures are from the author's book.

Grand Canyon & Surrounding Area

Grand Canyon N.P. Area Attractions You Must See
By William C. McElroy
Copyright 2007-2018

ISBN 9781654801786

Grand Canyon Area

The Grand Canyon area abounds in ancient and recent North American history, 800-plus year old ruins of the original Americas, endless canyons, lakes, rivers, flora, and life.

There are over a dozen Federal and State parks, and several Native American Reservations.

The Grand Canyon is near Flagstaff, a university town that support several Native American craft type stores.

Cameron Trading Post

From Flagstaff go north on Route 89 to *Cameron, Arizona* and spend 45 minutes searching the shelves for trinkets and Native American items.

Cameron Trading Post is an authentic Native American Indian trading post and lodge offering Grand Canyon hotel lodging along with Southwest and Native American works of art and jewelry, as well as the restaurant, lodge, and gift shop there is an art gallery. The Trading Post was built next to a suspension bridge that spans the

Little Colorado River. Cameron is on Route 89 just north of Route 64 junction and is a popular tourist stopping point

Homolovi Ruins State Park

Homolovi Ruins State Park now serves as a center of research for the late migration period of the Hopi from the 1200s to the late 1300s. While *archaeologists* study the sites and confer with the *Hopi* to unravel the history of Homolovi, the Arizona State Parks commission provides visitors the opportunity to visit the sites and use park facilities including a visitor center and museum, various trails and a campground.

"Homolovi" is Hopi for "Place of the Little Hills" — the traditional name for *Winslow, Arizona.*

From Flagstaff take I-40 E east 61.8 mi, take exit 257 for AZ-87 N toward Second Mesa 0.4 mi, turn left at 40/AZ-87/Historic US Route 66/E Second St (signs for AZ-87 N/Second Mesa) continue to follow AZ-87 1.5 mi, turn left at Honani Rd.

Hualapai Indian Reservation

West of the Grand Canyon lies the *Hualapai Native American Indian Reservation* and it is the new tourist spot for the American Southwest. The natives for many years have had dirt-poor living conditions and the community was very poor. Some time ago the natives decided to do something to help themselves and found that they could sell tourist on taking *rafting trips* down the *Colorado River* to *Lake Mead.* The trips begin with a bus ride down into the *Grand Canyon* along a dry creek, when it is not raining or flooded out. At the bottom of the canyon there are natives who suit you up in life vest and then give you the ride of your life down through the canyon and over rapids. The end of the day results in a *helicopter ride* up the shear walls of the canyon to the *Grand Canyon West Airport* terminal where you will catch a bus back to the *Hualapai village*.

The Hualapai village supports a very fine *motel* and restaurant combination *(Shown)*, a small park, some railroad tracks, dogs, cacti, and several dozen homes. Please respect the rules and regulations of no alcoholic beverages, and respect the privacy of the people and their homes and customs.

The newest addition to the Hualapai Reservation is the *"Glass 'U'"* walkway (Skywalk) that ventures out over the side of the Grand Canyon and provides an astonishing view of the size and depth of the canyon; you feel as if you are walking on air almost ¾ of a mile above the canyon floor. *(Grand Canyon Skywalk not shown, opened in March 2007)*

There are also *helicopter* flights to the rest area at the canyon floor, and for a small fee you can drop down and visit the Colorado River and the magnificence of the majestic canyon. *(Shown is the rest area at the end of the rafting where one waits for the helicopter to take him or her to the top of the ridge and the bus back to the Reservation)*

If you take a rafting trip through the canyon, then you may get a bus ride down into the launching spot and a helicopter ride up and out of the canyon. This helicopter is run by the

Hualapai Native Americans and will take people down to the river and back for a fee.

Montezuma's Castle

This hillside village is built into the mountain and is located south of Flagstaff off of I-17. It is a prime example of how some of the Natives to America lived hundreds of years ago. The valley was used for hunting, fishing, and growing crops, but the housing was built on the cliff side so that it required ladders to climb and enter each. This kept out the intruders that were not wanted or invited, and gave the people living here a military advantage over those that would try to conquer.

There is a small visitor center and museum, and there are several reasonably flat well-paved and marked walkways around the site, therefore it is handicap and wheelchair accessible.

Ground squirrels are abundant and each will beg for food making for some good close up photo taking. Shown is the favorite pose of many "men", that of holding up the building. Women get a kick out of us, but take the picture.

Montezuma's Castle is approximately 50 miles south of Flagstaff, Arizona and is off of I-17 at exit 298 just below McGuireville.

Montezuma's Well – Look Down

This small sunken pool of water *(Shown)* is located off of I-17 not far from *Montezuma's Castle*, and is a good place to visit. The water is clear and there are a variety of plants and animals that surround it, and feed from it.   What is not shown is the ancient Native American homes that are built into the walls of the *sinkhole* to the lower right of the person, me, in the picture; most people do not see these and are disappointed in the site, but if you take the time to look, then you will see all sorts of history, animals, and other life forms. The path to the Well is several hundred feet in length and winds through the desert flora, which is well labeled by small placards, take the time to read and learn about the desert and its bounty.

The park service has changed the original lookout area so that visitors can now better see the homes that are below the ridge.

The well is a limestone sinkhole caused by the ceiling of an ancient cavern collapse. The *Hohokam* and *Sinagua Indians* to water their crops used the water from the well *and old irrigation ditches can still be detected in the area. There is a Hohokam pithouse* and some remains of the Sinaguan *pueblos* left by the 150 to 200 natives that once resided there.

The path back to the parking entry location is now mostly paved and does go downhill for a distance. There is also a short offshoot path through a wooded area that is open for exploration. Total walk is about a mile and will take about 20 minutes; watch out for snakes sunning on the pavement.

Montezuma's Well is approximately 50 miles south of Flagstaff, Arizona off of I-17 at McGuireville, exit 293 onto Cornville Road going east.

Museum of Northern Arizona

Just north of the city of *Flagstaff, Arizona* is the *Museum of Northern Arizona* where you can view some of the artifacts of the *Native American Culture* that once inhabited the area. Plan to spend at least two hours in the museum.

The museum of Northern Arizona is located on highway Route 180 and is on one of the two possible routes to or from the *Grand Canyon* at Flagstaff.

Newspaper Rock

There are more than one Newspaper Rock sites in the desert Southwest; one is at the southern entry to *Canyonlands National Park,* and this one *(Shown)* is in the *Painted Desert.*

The American Indian natives hundreds of years ago traveled the desert on routes known to them, and in doing so had places along the trails where *"graffiti"* and other written communications could be presented and read; thus the name *"Newspaper Rock"*.

The rocks have what is termed *"Desert Varnish"* on each; Desert Varnish turns the surface of the rock black. By scratching into the varnish, the person could remove it and thus, leaving a tan-white impression. These impressions were mostly a symbolic language of the past, or then present, or possibly then future events and warnings to other travelers of the trails, and due to the longevity of the desert varnish these messages are still visible today, hundreds of years after being written, drawn.

Slide Rock State Park

Slide Rock State Park is just slightly north of Sedona and contains some great views of the majestic mountains there. *(Shown)*

Slide Rock State Park in the heart of *Oak Creek Canyon* features a natural *water slide* eroded into a slick creek bed, which is surrounded by massive red-rock walls. The slide makes this park a family favorite. The 43-acre park also includes a beautiful orchard and historic barn.

Just north of Slide Rock State Park the road winds upward to the top of the mountains and then further to *Flagstaff.*

The ride has several turnoff areas where you can pull over and relax for a period; and you may find that some of the Native Americans have set up camp at these turn offs and are selling *silver, turquoise,* and *gold* trinkets and *jewelry.* The prices are reasonable, and the quality is good, but be careful of those that pretend to be Native Americans and are selling cheap *Chinese or Mexican made goods.*

Hollywood movies such as "Broken Arrow" (1950) with James Stewart, "Drum Beat" (1954) with Alan Ladd and Charles Bronson, "Gun Fury" (1953) with Rock Hudson and Donna Reed, and a scene from "Angel and the Badman" (1946) with John Wayne were all shot at Slide Rock State Park. Note that in summer the park is very popular and the road, Route 89A at the entry of the park frequently backs up causing traffic jams and park entry closures.

Slide Rock State Park, 6871 N. Highway 89A, Sedona, AZ 86336

Tuzigoot National Monument (Sinagua Indian ruins)

Box 68, Clarkdale, AZ 86324

http://nps.gov/tuzi

Excavated ruins of large *Indian pueblo* that flourished in the *Verde Valley* between 1000 and 1400 A.D. The park is for day use only and there are the visitor center, *ruins*, and Indian exhibits.

This monument is not part of the Grand Canyon, but if you are traveling from *Flagstaff to Phoenix* it is a delightful side trip and well worth the extra hour or two. The ruins are high up on a hill overlooking a rich valley. At one time in the 1125 to 1400 period the pueblo housed approximately 200 natives. The main occupation of the people was hunting and farming and since many areas of the Southwest were in a drought the green valley village grew to overflowing. The Sinagua were excellent pottery makers and traded pottery to other tribes in the Southwest.

The ridge is high above the *Verde Valley*, and the original structure was two stories in height and had 77 ground-floor rooms. There were ceremonial chambers and a dump; the dump proved valuable in determining the occupants and their lifestyle as many pieces of broken pottery was discovered in it.

The name *Tuzigoot is Apache* for *"Crooked Waters"* and the village sat on the ridge that is 120 feet above the valley floor, and thus offered a good defense for the occupants who could see any enemy coming for miles.

Tuzigoot is off of route 89A and 279 near *Clarkdale, Arizona* and should be part of any trip to *Montezuma Castle*, *Montezuma Well, Camp Verde State Historic Park*, and *Jerome State Historic Park. Fort Verde* is an 1871 fort, and Jerome is the home of one of the first *copper mines* in Arizona.

Location: 48 miles southwest of Flagstaff, off U.S. 89A. If you did not want to go to Tuzigoot from *Montezuma's Castle*, then go north on I-17 to exit 298 and turn north on Route 179 to *Sedona, Arizona* or stay on I-17 north to *Flagstaff, Arizona*.

Accommodations: Meals and lodging in Clarkdale and *Cottonwood, Arizona*, 2 miles from the monument

A slightly longer ride will take one to the Canyon de Chelly (Shay) National Park. The *Walnut Canyon National Monument* Indian ruins are 12-miles east of Flagstaff, and are well worth the visit.

Walnut Canyon National Monument

In the pine forests near *Flagstaff, Arizona*, is a steep canyon that severs the rolling plateaus. Twenty miles long, 400 feet deep and ¼-mile wide, *Walnut Creek* carved it over a period of 60 million years. Within its winding walls are natural riches – an abundant mix of plants and animals drawn there by water and varied topography.

Built by *Pueblo Indians* about 800 years ago are the *Cliff dwellings* in shallow caves under limestone ledges. Access to cliff dwellings is a steep set of rugged steps and it is a hardy walk.

The Walnut Canyon National Monument contains *Pueblo* and *Pithouse ruins*, and several trails that overlook the Walnut Creek canyon. There is a Visitor Center and there is a picnic area. The canyon differs from most of the Arizona area in that it is tree lined and mostly green. The ancient natives lived in the area from about 1100 to 1250.

The *Island Trail* descends 185 feet (56 m) into the canyon providing access to *25 cliff dwelling rooms*. A strenuous .9-mile (1.4 km) round trip, this is one of the best ways to experience the park. The elevation is 6,690ft (2,039 meters) and climbing the 240 steps back up can tax the heart and lungs, so bring water and rest frequently. The Island Trail closes one hour before the visitor center closes.

14

The *Rim Trail* (.7 mi/1km) offers an easy overview of the canyon. The Rim Trail closes 30 minutes before the visitor center.

Accommodations: Meals and lodging are in Flagstaff. The park's visitor center, cliff dwellings, self-guiding trail, and picnic area are for day use only.

If driving from Flagstaff, leave I-40 at Exit 204, 7.5 miles (12 km) east of Flagstaff; drive south 3 miles (5 km) to the canyon rim. Warning: Tight turn-around in parking area for towed vehicles; 40 feet (12 meters) maximum length is recommended.

Wupatki National Monument

Sunset Crater Volcano National Monument
Route 3, Box 149, Flagstaff, AZ 86004

The park is connected to *Wupatki National Monument* by a paved road that runs through the *Coconino National Forest*. A Forest Service campground is located across from the visitor center.

Wupatki National Monument

Ruins of masonry pueblos built by *Sinagua* and *Anasazi Indian farmers* between A.D. 100 and 1225 are part of a complex *prehistoric* story of struggle for survival in a harsh climate. The site contains a Visitor center, ruins, self-guiding trails, and a picnic area; it is connected to *Sunset Crater National Monument* by paved road leading from *Coconino National Forest*.

There are five sets of pueblo ruins at the park and shown is the first of the five at the Visitor Center. The second is the *Wukoki Pueblo*, and the third through fifth are further onward and near the end of the Loop Road.

Did You Know?
The large pueblos preserved at Wupatki National Monument were constructed in the years following the eruption of nearby Sunset Crater, sometime between 1040 and 1100. *Volcanic ash*, deposited in thin layers, retained moisture and improved farming that brought in people from miles distant, and thus increased the population at Wupatki.

Take 89 north out of Flagstaff to the turnoff (right turn) onto *Loop Road* (the loop is about 35 miles total), this will get you to the *Sunset Crater Volcano National Monument* where you can stop in the Visitors Center for pictures, information, etc.

Continue on Loop Road to the *Painted Desert Vista*, and then onward to *Wupatki Pueblo Visitor Center*. The *Wukoki Pueblo* is to the right of the center back a hundred feet from the center, and the *Wupatki Pueblo* is to the left of the center on a half-mile looping trail. When finished, continue on the Loop Road to the *Box Canyon Dwelling*, and the *Nalakihu, Citadel,* and *Lomaki Pueblos*. From there continue along Loop Road to Route 89 and turn left to go back to *Flagstaff*. The entire loop takes about 35 to 50 minutes to drive, but plan on two to four hours if you are to visit each vista and pueblo.

16

Box Canyon Dwelling

Formation of *Box Canyon* (Shown) is believed to have been by an ancient earthquake that split the land. The story is

that the nearby Native Indians used the canyon as a *"freezer"* by filling it with snow and ice during the winter months. They are reported to have placed their "kills" of deer and animals into the snow mix and allowed each to freeze, and since the canyon is deep and receives little sunlight, it kept the meat frozen well into the late spring months.

Nalakihu, Citadel, and Lomaki Pueblos

Near the ruins of these pueblos is a gigantic *sinkhole* caused by the collapse of a large underground *limestone cave (Shown).* You will have to park your vehicle at the road

and walk up the hillside to the ruins where you can view the sinkhole, the *San Francisco Peaks* forty miles away, and the *Sunset Crater* fourteen miles distant.

Location: Off U.S. 89, 45 miles north of *Flagstaff.*
Accommodations: Meals and lodging in Flagstaff.

HC33, Box 444A, Flagstaff, AZ 86001

The following text is from the authors book "100+ Tucson and Vicinity Attractions"

Amerind Museum

American Indians from all the Americas, including North, South, and Central America. Amer = Americas, ind = Indian

This museum is in two buildings, each with two floors. The first building contains artifacts and costumes of Native Americans from South, Central, and North America.

The second building, (shown) has artwork from various artists that are prominent in southwestern artworks. There is a path near this building that goes to a restroom and picnic area and some very big

Texas Canyon rock formations. Worth the extra 30-minute walk; wear good walking shoes, sunscreen, and a hat. Watch for snakes.

Plan on spending from two to four hours at this location.

Amerind Museum, 2100 N Amerind Road, Dragoon, AZ 85609 – GPS 32.045585, -110.078648

Arizona Historical Society Museum

Close to the University of Arizona and downtown Tucson is this history museum that features the history of Tombstone, mining, brick manufacturing, past Indian wars, an Indian Village, antiques,

paintings, and even a vehicle or two. Worth the low admission price and you can spend from two to six hours to see all the displays

Arizona History Museum, 949 E 2nd Street, Tucson, AZ 85719 - GPS 32.233366, -110.957333 (Park at 885-815 E 2nd Street)

Arizona State Museum

This museum is unique as it takes you on a journey through the history of the Native Americans of the American Southwest.

It is unfortunate that parking is a few blocks distant, but the walk to the museum is relaxing and the museum is a treasure to enjoy. You will follow the hallways past Native American history during your two to three hour journey.

Best place to park is 885-815 E 2nd Street, Tucson, AZ 85719 - GPS 32.233006, -110.958815

Casino del Sol

The Native American Tribe has two (2) casinos with almost the same name. There is the Casino of the Sun (Casino del Sol) shown, and there is the Casino del Sol (Casino of the Sun) not shown.

The Valencia Road location has a golf course, hotel, restaurants, gaming halls, outdoor concert area, and fireworks on the 4th of July and New Years (Check first).

The Camino De Oeste location has a snack bar and gaming and is used by many of the locals.

Casino Del Sol, 5655 W Valencia Road, Tucson, AZ 85757 - GPS 32.131050, -111.086901

Chiricahua Regional Museum

This small but interesting museum has Cowboy and Indian artifacts, costumes, and history.

The museum has items of the old west that are unique and not normally shown in other western museums.

Plan on spending an hour at this location.

Chiricahua (Chair-I-cow-ah) Regional Museum, 127 E Maley Street, Willcox, AZ 85643 - GPS 32.252359, -109.831398

Desert Diamond Casino

There are two locations for gaming. Native Americans own these and you will be on reservation land.

The Sahuarita (Saa-re-ta) location off of I-19 south of Tucson has gaming and a large showroom that features name entertainment weekly. There is plenty of free parking and lots of food and drink available.

The Nogales (No-gal-us) location has gaming and the hotel; it is a few miles north of the Sahuarita location.

Desert Diamond Casinos & Entertainment, Sahuarita, 1100 W Pima Mine Road, Sahuarita, AZ 85629 - GPS 32.005612, -110.988107

Fort Bowie

Apache Spring is a water source for the area and it is one of the prime reasons for the creation of Fort Bowie; the second prime reason was that the Butterfield Stage ran through the valley and the fort was assigned to protect it.

There were many battles and therefore you will gain knowledge of the history as you walk the 1.5 miles from the parking area to the top of the mountain and the NPS Visitor Center. On your walk you will pass the remains of the Butterfield Stage station, the cemetery (shown), many foundations, an Indian encampment, and the Apache Spring.

At the visitor center you will find uniforms, artwork, weapons, and the foundations of the main encampment. For those that cannot hike the 1.5 miles on the dirt path and up the mountain, there is a parking area several hundred feet down the slope from the visitor center, but you need NPS permission to use it. There is a restroom at the parking area and the visitor center, but no other facilities, thus bring food, water, sunscreen, and good walking shoes.

The road to the parking area is dirt, it is long, and it passes the *Wagon Massacre Site* as well as some other markers. The path up to the NPS visitor center is dirt and in some areas steep, thus do not attempt unless in good physical shape. Behind the visitor center is another path, it can be used to go back down the mountain to the parking area.

Watch for snakes, and for deer as this is wilderness and you might encounter one or both on your hike.

Plan on four to eight hours round trip from Willcox.

Fort Bowie National Historic Site, 3500 Apache Pass Road, Bowie, AZ 85605 – GPS 32.156562, -109.452661

Fort Bowie Ranger Station & Visitor Center, Bowie, AZ 85605 – GPS 32.145868, -109.436399

Mission San Xavier del Bac

The mission at Tucumcari has been left 'raw' by the NPS. It shows the rough structure of a Spanish Mission built decades ago. This mission has been restored to show the contrast, and therefore you should visit both.

Plenty of parking, lots of Native American food via local vendors, gift and book stores, a small mountain hike, seasonal Pow Wows, and some of the best mission reconstruction you will see are at this south Tucson facility. Note you are on Native American property and they do have their police and laws, thus show proper respect.

There is a school next door, and a graveyard along the roadway, no pictures of the graves are permitted, but pictures in the mission are encouraged. They do have church services on Sundays and you will not be permitted in the main church for 'sightseeing'.

Mission San Xavier del Bac Indian Reservation, San Xavier Road, Tucson, Arizona - GPS 32.106682, -111.008372

Chapter # 04 – California:

The following text and pictures are from the author's book.

The California / Oregon / Nevada Loop
Copyright August 2018 - 2021,
William (Bill) C. McElroy

ISBN: 9798725229530

All photos unless otherwise marked are the exclusive properties of the copyright owner and may not be copied, modified, or otherwise duplicated.

Del Norte County Historical Society

.8 mile, 4 minutes

From the *delnortehistory.org* website

"The Main Museum has a wealth of interesting displays. One room is devoted to artifacts of the local Tolowa and Yurok Native Americans. It includes one of the finest Native American basket collections in Northern California. Musical instruments, old radio, phonographic and photographic equipment, excellent needlework, early logging and mining tools and equipment, and many fashions and furniture from yesteryear are just some of the objects and subjects represented and on display in the Main Museum."

"The Bolen Annex houses the magnificent First Order Fresnel Lens from the Saint George Reef Lighthouse."

Del Norte County Historical Society, 577 H Street, Crescent City, CA 95531 - GPS 41.754243, -124.199298

Fort Humboldt State Historic Park

15.7 miles, 20 minutes

From *parks.ca.gov* website

"Fort Humboldt was formally abandoned in 1870 and rapidly fell into decay. Today, only the hospital building remains of the original fourteen structures. It is now an historical museum dedicated to telling the story of the Fort and the Native American groups, including the

{Wikipedia photo by JP Smith, it is Public Domain}

Wiyot, Hoopa and Yurok of this region. In the 1980's the Surgeon's Quarters was reconstructed and there are plans for its establishment as a period house museum. In 2001 an historic herb and vegetable garden was recreated adjacent to the Hospital."

"Fort Humboldt SHP Logging Artifacts The park also includes a Logging Museum and open air displays of historic 19th-mid 20th century logging equipment including the Dolbeer Steam Donkey; "Lucy," the Bear Harbor Lumber Company's Gypsy Locomotive #1; and the Elk River Mill and Lumber Company's #1 "Falk" locomotive."

Plan on two to three hours.

Fort Humboldt State Historic Park, 3431 Fort Ave, Eureka, CA 95503 - GPS 40.776848, -124.188548

Fortuna Depot Museum

8.3 miles, 13 minutes

{Photo from the friendlyfortuna.com website}

From the Fortuna Website
"Featured displays include railroad and logging artifacts, a collection of local Native American basketry, a general store display, the Arden Taylor/Vernon Dahl fishing collection, a 4 ½ foot diameter copper Swiss cheese cauldron, and the Al Rogers collection of barbed wire, tools, locks, and 156 antique spark plugs. There are also 4-6 seasonally changing exhibits each year, as well as month-long temporary displays installed by members of Fortuna's Relic Accumulators' Club. "

Plan on 30 minutes to an hour.

Fortuna Depot Museum, 3 Park Street, Fortuna, CA 95540 - GPS 40.599485, -124.149495

Santa Ynez Valley Historical Museum and Parks-Janeway Carriage House

28.6 miles, 38 minutes

This small museum shows the history of the Santa Ynez valley and its inhabitants from the Chumash Indians to today's populations.

From Wikipedia

> *"The Chumash are a Native American people who historically inhabited the central and southern coastal regions of California, in portions of what is now San Luis Obispo, Santa Barbara, Ventura and Los Angeles counties, extending from Morro Bay in the north to Malibu in the south. They also occupied three of the Channel Islands: Santa Cruz, Santa Rosa, and San Miguel; the smaller island of Anacapa was likely inhabited seasonally due to the lack of a consistent water source"*

The carriage house has horse drawn carriages on display. See their website *santaynezmuseum.org* for a photo.

Plan on 45 minute to an hour or so for viewing this museum.

Santa Ynez Valley Historical Museum and Parks-Janeway Carriage House, 3596 Sagunto Street, Santa Ynez, CA 93460 - GPS 34.612528, -120.080215

The following text and pictures are from the author's book

Death Valley Visitors Guide
By
William (Bill) C. McElroy
ISBN 9781089151593
Copyright 2016-2018

Indian Village

Approximately 50 members of the Native American Timbisha Shoshone Tribe live in Indian Village. This is their home; it is not open to the general public

Location and Directions to:
South of Furnace Creek, California at GPS 36.453012,-116.863718 is the road, Tumpisa Loop, which goes into Indian Village, California, GPS 36.449387,-116.874153

Shoshone Castles or Castles in Clay

These are cave homes carved out of the clay mountain area east of the California town of Shoshone. The homes were probably that of Native Americans from long ago.

At one time and according to Wikipedia:

"In California the Timbisha Shoshone (also known as the Death Valley or Panamint Shoshone) have lived for centuries in the Death Valley, Saline Valley, Panamint Valley and surrounding

mountains. They have a federally recognized tribal reservation and government at Furnace Creek, California. In 1933 President Herbert Hoover created Death Valley National Monument, an action that subsumed the tribe's homeland within park boundaries."

"Despite their long-time presence in the region, the proclamation failed to provide a homeland for the Timbisha people. After unsuccessful efforts to remove the band to nearby reservations, National Park Service officials entered into an agreement with tribal leaders to allow the Civilian Conservation Corps to construct an Indian village for tribal members near park headquarters at Furnace Creek in 1938."

{ GPS 35°58'23"N 116°16'16"W }

Chapter # 05 – Colorado:

Tribes

"There are two federally recognized Tribes in Colorado, the Southern Ute Indian Tribe and the Ute Mountain Ute Tribe. Each of the Tribes has a constitution, code of laws, and court system that are separate and independent of state and local governments."

https://ccia.colorado.gov/tribes

https://www.cde.state.co.us/sites/default/files/documents/cdereval/download/pdf/race-ethnicity/nativeamericantribesofcolorado.pdf

Cortez, Colorado

Hovenweep National Monument, Location: 45 miles from Cortez, Colo., on Utah-Colorado border. GPS 37.383734,-109.072587, gets you to the park buildings and the Campground areas. Be prepared to do some walking, the ruins are in the canyons northwest of the parking area.

Mancos, Colorado

Mesa Verde National Park, State Highway 10 & U.S. 160, Mancos, CO 81328
The entry road is at GPS 37.340223,-108.411734 and it is a ride on a very twisting road up a mountain and down the other side. Be patient, you will get there, and you will be thrilled that you took the day to drive from ***Monticello, Utah*** where you are staying for a few days so you can visit ***Canyonlands (Newspaper rock), Arches, and National Bridges National parks***.

Manitou Springs, Colorado

Manitou Cliff Dwellings
10 Cliff Rd, Manitou Springs, CO 80829
38.862810, -104.912996

Cañon Pintado

"Cañon Pintado, meaning painted canyon, is an archaeological site of Native American rock art located in the East Four Mile Draw, 10.5 miles (16.9 km) south of Rangely in Rio Blanco County, Colorado. Led by Ute guides, the Domínguez–Escalante expedition, Spanish missionaries in search of a route to California in 1776, passed through this region as they moved north and then west into Utah. The first Europeans to the area, they named it Cañon Pintado, meaning "painted canyon".

Restricted access.

https://en.wikipedia.org/wiki/Ca%C3%B1on_Pintado

Chapter # 06 – New Mexico:

The following text and pictures are from the author's book.

The Guide to Touring New Mexico
By
William (Bill) C. McElroy
Copyright 2016-2018
ISBN 9798713738235

Acoma Pueblo

This pueblo (Native American town) is the home of the *Sky City Cultural Center/Haak'u Museum.* The town is considered to be the '*Enchanted Mesa*' or '*Sky City*' home of the *San Esteban del Rey Mission.* Plan on two to five hours visiting this site.

The Pueblo is about 12 miles south of I-40 Exit 108, but should be on your list of places to see, just obey the rules as this is a Native American site. ~ 34.896738,-107.581902

Cebolleta Historical Marker
Acoma Pueblo, NM 87034
34.896437, -107.581994

Dinosaur Rock
Acoma Pueblo, NM 87034
34.896208, -107.585900

San Estevan del Rey Mission Church Historic Site
Acoma Pueblo, NM 87034
34.895325, -107.582385

Sky City Cultural Center/Haak'u Museum
Haaku Road, Acoma Pueblo, NM 87034
34.901589, -107.587961

Ashiwi Awan Museum & Heritage

A small group established this museum in 1992; it displays the heritage of the Zuni peoples and their history. Plan on one to two hours at this location.

2E Ojo Caliente Road,
Zuni, NM 87327
35.066051, -108.851759

Aztec Mill Museum (Open in the Summer)

Museum is a collection of items from the local area and some of its past residents. The museum building was originally a Civil War Flour Mill that served Fort Sumner that was detaining Jicarilla Apaches and Navajos.   Museum is closed in the winter months. Plan on spending one to two hours.

W 17th Street,
Cimarron, NM 87714
36.504854, -104.922581

Aztec Museum & Pioneer Village

The one-room schoolhouse and the Denver & Rio Grande Railroad caboose are among the items that date from around 1900 to date. The museum is handicap accessible and has free parking. Nearby are the Aztec ruins, and miles to the southwest are the Chaco ruins. Other buildings at the museum and pioneer village are a tinsmith, print shop, carpentry shop, church, magistrate judge office, post office, general store, doctor's office, and an old Aztec jail. Plan on from two to six hours at this location.

125 N Main Ave,
Aztec, NM 87410
36.823423, -107.994842

Aztec Ruins National Monument

This National Monument is an Ancestral Puebloan site where you can walk the trail while listening on your phone to the descriptions of what you are seeing. There is a reconstructed Great Kiva, and if you do not have a Smart phone, then ask for the laminated guide booklet. Plan on one to two hours.

36.834406,-108.000616
70 Road 2900, Aztec, NM 87410

Aztec, New Mexico

Aztec Ruins National Monument,
Location: Outskirts of small northwestern New Mexico city of Aztec. GPS 36.834342,-108.000632

Bandelier National Monument

{Cliff homes, Wikipedia, Public Domain}

If you decide to visit Los Alamos and its museums then also plan on spending an hour or two at the Bandelier National Monument with its ancient Cliff Dwellings and nature walk. This site has a foundation of an Indian pueblo, a small museum, a very large gift shop, and several dwelling caves that are high on the cliffs. There are ladders to the caves that you can climb to see how our ancestral Native Americans lived hundreds of years ago. Take the nature walk as it goes downhill to a small brook, and then double back to the parking lot; serene and peaceful.

15 Entrance Road,

Bandelier National Monument,
Los Alamos, NM 87544.
35.778802,-106.270237

Bandelier National Monument,

15 Entrance Road, Bandelier National Monument, Los Alamos, NM 87544 near the top of the mountain by *Los Alamos National Laboratory* where the *Atomic Bomb* was developed (*Los Alamos Museum* closed on certain days and hours).

Park is located at GPS 35.778767,-106.270334; you are required to park in the lot, enter the ticket and museum building, and then walk the tour. Most of the walk is reasonably flat, but for those that wish, there is a mountain path to the right that takes you up to the *Cave Houses on the Cliffs*. Wooden ladders are provided for those that want to enter a Cave House. The remainder of the trail snakes down through the woods past a stream and back to your car. Food, drink, and gifts are available there.

Blackwater Draw Museum

This museum features anthropology and the study of ancients like the Clovis People that once roamed the hills and valleys of New Mexico and the American southwest. Artifacts displayed may date back as far as 12,000 to 13,500 years

1457-1461 S Avenue K,
Portales, NM 88130
34.175819, -103.346912

Canyon de Chelly National Monument,

Location: From Gallup, N. Mex., northwest on U.S. 666 to N. Mex. 264 to U.S. 191 to Chinle and then to the park at GPS 36.152898,-109.539227. Do the South Rim Drive first, then the North Rim Drive, if you still have time. Make sure you stop at the Park Headquarters for refreshments, a peek at what you will see, and a park map. Most of the viewpoint areas are walkable; but some are not or may be difficult for those with impairments.

Chaco Culture National Historical Park,

Location: N. Mex. 57 in northwestern New Mexico, 64 miles south of Aztec, N. Mex. GPS 36.028599,-107.904067 is the main in/out entry point, the entire complex is large and there is a one-way road the circles the main ruins that can be visited. Roads are a mix of pavement and dirt, check with NPS for details and local weather before making the long trip into the site. Plan on a full day.

Casinos

New Mexico's Native American citizens from Albuquerque to Santa Fe have several casino resorts that you can frequent while in the area. There are road signs all along the highway that will direct you to each.

Native American Ruins

Directions are provided from the nearest major town to the site's entry points, using best possible roads.

There may be other entry points on other roads, but many are remote and not paved, thus requiring something other than the family car.

Picture, prayer service at the *Wounded Knee Reservation Gravesite.* No, it is not in New Mexico but rather in South Dakota.

Chief Yellowhorse Trading Post

Commercial establishment that has become somewhat of a tourist stop nestled in a crevice in the hillside along I-40.

Dream catchers, headdresses, rain sticks, Turquoise jewelry, pottery, Kachina Dolls, Navajo Fry bread, blankets, and much, much more are available at this Native American Trading Post. Be aware of what you do purchase, as throughout the southwest there are original and genuine Native American items and there are copies from China and Mexico that do not fit the 'original and genuine' category.

I-40 Exit 359 just over the border from New Mexico into Arizona. There are several Native American sales booths at this exit as well as food, gasoline, a rest area, the tourist center, and a spot for great pictures. Plan on 15 minutes to an hour.

Yellowhorse Trading Post & More
359 I-40,
Lupton, AZ 86508
35.358893, -109.052338

El Morro National Monument

NM-53, Ramah, NM 87321
{Park featuring over 2,000 signatures carved into sandstone, dating back to ancient Pueblo times}
35.039670, -108.345074

El Morro National Monument Visitor Center

Highway 53, Ramah, NM 87321
35.038642, -108.348954

Fort Craig National Historic Site

In the 1867 to 1869 period the Buffalo Soldiers were stationed at Fort Craig and while there they helped to capture Billy the Kid and Gerónimo. Today there is a small museum showing the history of the fort, and there are some walls and foundations of the various buildings. Plan on an hour at this location.

Fort Craig National Historic Site
Ft Craig Road,
San Antonio, NM 87832
33.635522, -107.016483

Frances Canyon Indian Ruins

This site contains many nearly intact ruins that date back to the 1680 period. These ruins are somewhat isolated from the main roads and do require a bit of doing, and hiking, to get to. Plan for four to six hours.

Placard on the site reads.

Frances Canyon Navajo Ruins
Navajo Dam, NM 87419
36.764884, -107.497925

Gerónimo Springs Museum

The Gerónimo Spring Museum has the history of how and why the town was named Truth or Consequences, and also the Hardcastle Cabin, the history of the Apache Native and Gerónimo, mastodon fossils, and branding irons. There is a gift shop. Plan on spending one to three hours.

211 Main Ave,
Truth or Consequences, NM 87901
33.130057, -107.252622

Gila Cliff Dwellings

From the Gila Trailhead Museum you will have about a 2,300-foot hike across the Gila River Bridge up the hillside, and along the cliffs to the cliff dwelling site. Plan on a minimum of one hour for the round trip hike and picture taking at the Mogollon-built cliff dwellings. Plan on one hour combined for each of the two museums

/ visitor centers. There are camping sites and other hiking trails at the park and thus, you can spend a day or more here.

Gila Trailhead Museum
Silver City, NM 88061
33.229410, -108.264852

Gila Visitor Center
Gila National Forest,
Silver City, NM 88061
33.223858, -108.241757

Hubbell Trading Post National Historic Site,

Location: This is on the Navajo' Indian Reservation, one mile west of Ganado, and 55 miles from Gallup. N. Mexico off of US 191 at GPS 35.710119,-109.552719.

Jemez and Jemez Springs, Pueblo

This small town has hot springs, shopping, fine motels, and is a vacation spot for many.

17599-17549 NM-4
Jemez Springs, NM 87025
35.770021, -106.691524

Jemez Monument (Native American Ruins)

{Jemez Historic Site}

This site has the foundations of about three-dozen rooms and the remains of the mission that you can enter and explore. If you went to Los Alamos or Bandelier then when leaving each go west to NM-4 and then south to the site. Staying on NM-4 will take you to US-555 and that will take you to I-25 and Santa Fe.

Jemez Historic Site
18160 NM-4,

Jemez Springs, NM 87025
35.778508, -106.686583

Kasha-Katuwe Tent Rocks National Monument

This is a short hike from the trailhead to the series of rock
formations that resemble Native American tents.

Jemez Springs, NM 87025
35.656652, -106.411149

Kiva

A Kiva is a Native American ceremonial room that is built in the
round and partly below ground. It is sacred to Native Americans
and although you may look inside, it is not normally allowed to
enter inside. Most of the Native American ancient ruins throughout
the American southwest have one or more Kiva.

Bernalillo, NM 87004
{This is one part of a Native American Ruin}

Kiva
Bernalillo, NM 87004
35.330150, -106.557558

Largo Canyon Indian Ruins

See *Frances Canyon Navajo Ruins* and *Abo Ruins* elsewhere in this
guide.

New Mexico - Map of Native America

This colorful map shows the General Location of the Native American Reservations, pueblos, missions, and ruin in the Albuquerque, Grant, and Santa Fe areas of New Mexico.

{I

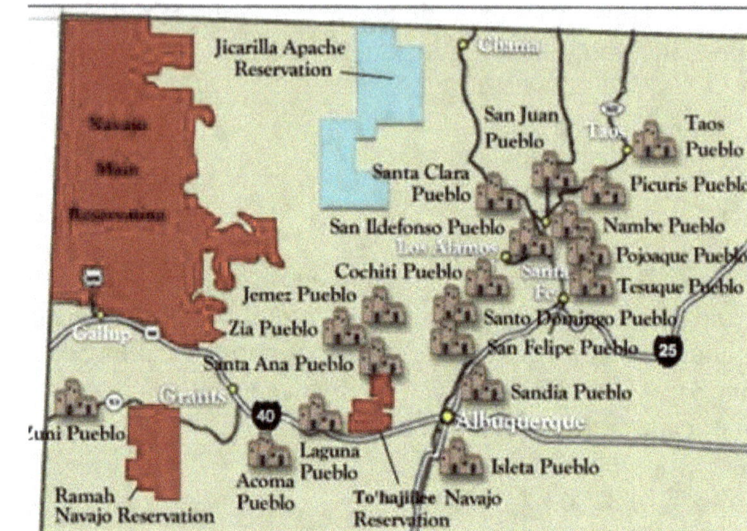

believe the picture is public domain from Wikipedia}

Petroglyph National Monument,

Location: *Visitor center* is located 3 miles north of I-40 on Unser Boulevard. The Visitor Center is at GPS 35.138388,-106.71087. Also go to GPS 35.167231,-106.724753 for the second section of the park, called *Boca Negra Canyon Trails*

St Joseph Apache Mission

This 1920 mission is just off of US-70 and is good for a 5-minute picture shoot.

626 Mission Road,
Mescalero, NM 88340
GPS 33.154987,-105.767548

Taos Pueblo

{Taos Pueblo postcard criteria 1930, Wikipedia, Public Domain}

This is a popular and famous touring spot that represents a portion of Native American. Not many places in the US can claim to be one of the oldest continuously occupied places in the US, but here a mile north of the town of Taos there is the Taos Pueblo.

This village is unique in that many of the homes can only be entered by ladder; a method of keeping unwanted visitors out of the living room. There is an old mission, a graveyard, and many buildings to see; Note…this is part of Native America and these are their homes and laws, so be respectful and ask before taking pictures, entering spaces, or climbing ladders. It is best to park your vehicle and walk the loop between the north and south homes. Plan on 30 minutes minimum.

Taos Pueblo
New Mexico
36.438585, -105.546964

The Chiricahua Desert Museum

This museum represents one of the best on herpetology (Study of reptiles and amphibians, i.e., snakes). It also features many items of the Native American occupation of the southwest, guns, wagons, and western pioneer items. Plan on one to two hours.

From the official website

The Chiricahua Desert Museum
NM-80 & Portal Road, Rodeo, NM 88056
31.870412, -109.034863

Three Rivers Petroglyph Site

Site has lots of Petroglyphs, some camping sites, a few RV sites, and a few Rattlesnakes just for good measure. Plan on a short but energetic hike of one to two hours.

Inhabitants of a nearby village made the Three River Petroglyphs (rock carving) over 600 years ago. Over 20,000 Petroglyphs have been identified in the area. The people were of the Jornada Mogollon (hor-NAH-da muggy-OWN) prehistoric Indian culture, of which there are no known modern descendants.

Tularosa, NM 88352

46

3.344711, -106.008671

Tularosa Basin Museum of History

The museum features lots of history of the area and both the pioneers and the Native American habitant that called it home for generations. There are wagons, arrowheads, pottery, typewriters, furniture, and much more to see. Plan for one-hour minimum.

1004 N White Sands Blvd,
Alamogordo, NM 88310
32.900113, -105.960015

Wheelwright Museum of the American Indian

{See Museum Hill write up}

Window Rock – Navajo Code Breakers Monument

On the road over to the Hubbell Trading post you will pass ***Window Rock*** at GPS 35.663398,-109.054499; this is where the ***Navajo Code Breakers Monument*** is; and there is a motel and restaurant there as well as a Navajo Zoo and Library (check for days and hours). The rooms at the motel are interesting and the food at the restaurant is good. Cows outside your door, but......

Note the Monument and Window Rock Park ***with Kiva*** is at GPS 35.680716,-109.049644.

Zia Pueblo

In 1583 Antonio de Espejo recorded this pueblo as one of five in the Province of Puname. Following the sacking of Zia by Spanish troops in 1698, the pueblo was reestablished, but never attained its former size. The Zia ancient sun symbol is incorporated in the design of the state flag of New Mexico.

NM 87053
~35.506229, -106.721674

Zuni Tourism Center

This tour center is where you purchase permits to photo the items, and homes in the village. You can learn about the history of the Zuni people and their customs, food items, cooking means, and much more. Worth 30 minutes to an hour.

Zuni Visitor Center
1231-1245 NM-53,
Zuni, NM 87327
35.071955, -108.840085

Chapter # 07 – Nevada:

https://nevadaindiancommission.org/map-of-nevada-tribes/

Nevada Indian Commission
5500 Snyder Avenue,
Building #3
Carson City, NV 89701
(775) 687-8333

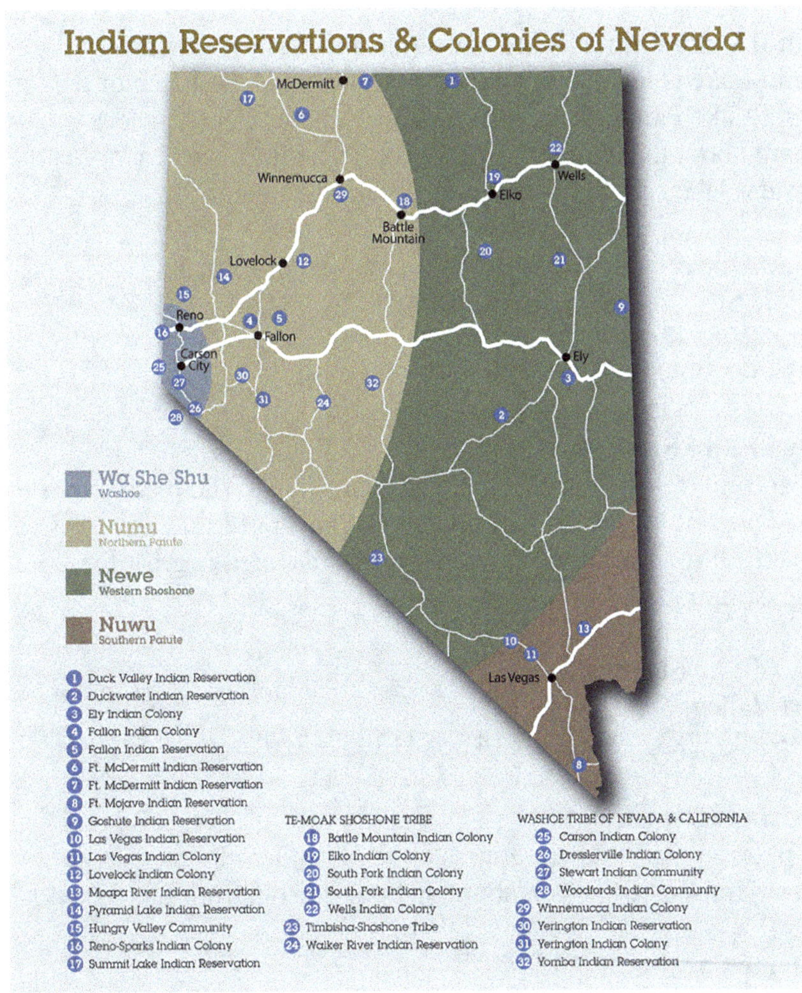

Lost City Museum

The Lost City Museum located in Overton, Nevada can provide lots of information about the lives of the Ancestral Puebloan people. These natives were skilled farmers, weavers, and potters. The museum features exhibits on the history and culture of the Puebloans, as well as artifacts that were excavated from the ruins of their villages.

Lost City Museum
721 S Moapa Valley Blvd,
Overton, NV 89040
GPS 36.531452337173896, -114.44086665766862

Pyramid Lake Paiute Tribe Museum and Visitor Center
Pyramid Lake is located in Nixon, Nevada and is the home of the Pyramid Lake Paiute Tribe Museum and Visitor Center where you can learn about this culture. In addition Pyramid Lake is a large freshwater lake suitable for fishing, swimming, etc.

Pyramid Lake Paiute Tribe Museum and Visitor Center
709 State St,
Nixon, NV 89424
39.822352859892575, -119.36569757116354

Valley of Fire State Park
You can find lots of Native American petroglyphs and pictographs at the Valley of Fire State Park that is just north of Las Vegas. There are beautiful red sandstone formations; and the area is great for hiking, camping, and rock climbing.

Valley of Fire State Park
Moapa Valley, NV 89040
GPS 36.47572831723855, -114.5384139576729

Grapevine Canyon
More petroglyphs and pictographs by the Southern Paiute can be found at Grapevine Canyon about an hour's drive from Las Vegas.

Grapevine Canyon
Christmas Tree Pass Road

Searchlight, NV 89046
GPS 35.22583450970968, -114.68162730874059

Clark County Museum

In Henderson, Nevada you can go to the Clark County Museum that
has some history of the Southern Paiute people and of Las Vegas.

Clark County Museum
1830 S Boulder Hwy,
Henderson, NV 89002
36.01007458519965, -114.94537864229683

Moapa Travel Center

You can purchase native crafts at the Moapa Travel Center, it is run
by the Moapa Band of Paiute peoples.

Moapa Travel Center
Valley of Fire Highway and I-15,
Moapa, NV 89025
GPS 36.499769126580574, -114.75957918647092

Lovelock Cave

In northwestern Nevada you may find the archaeological site known
as Lovelock Cave. The artifacts, mummies, baskets, and such date
back thousands of years. This is not a well marked or an easy to get
to location, and it is a cave with a stairway down into it. There are
placards and a parking area, but you will do some hiking.

GPS 39.962504023271826, -118.5582627576694

Chapter # 08 – South Dakota:

The following text and pictures are from the author's book

Explore South Dakota's Many, Many, Attractions
By William (Bill) C. McElroy
Copyright
ISBN 9798713785666

Akta Lakota Museum & Cultural Center

Museum features the history of the Lakota by oldest dates to the newest. There is a small gift shop, and there is a church (Our Lady of the Sioux). It is family friendly and worth an hour or so of your time when in the area.

1301 N Main Street, Chamberlain, SD 57325
43.825310, -99.324774

Cheyenne River Sioux Cultural Center

Cheyenne River Cultural Center
AKA – *Harry V Johnston Lakota Cultural Center*
Eagle Butte, SD 57625
45.007484, -101.228641

Crazy Horse Memorial (Must See)

As one drives north on Route #16/385, he or she will see a carving on a distant mountain to the right, and if you did not know better, the first reaction is 'is that *Mount Rushmore*'?

Nope, it is not, but it is the *Crazy Horse Memorial*, a cliff carving that started decades ago and will probably take decades to complete, if ever.

The idea was to help the *Native Americans* of the area

gain employment, schooling, and recognition; the result is a full-scale tourist attraction that generates a million or so each year for the children of its creator, non-American Indians.

There is a huge gift shop and restaurant, with movie theater in the main building. From here one purchases tickets to ride a bus up to the bottom of the mountain where the workmen are drilling, laying in dynamite, blowing chunks off the mountain, and then chipping away to smooth the surface into portions of the massive structure.

There are also some outside statues and exhibits, one of which is a scale model that is housed out of the weather and comes out on rails when enough people are searching for a peek.

Inside and toward the rear of the main building is a sales area for the Native Americans that live in the area;

There are about a dozen tables adorned with Native American *jewelry*, paintings, costumes, and such. There are also a few displays for the tourist to look upon and take a photo or two.

The *classrooms* that were to be used for education for the Native Americans are not built and therefore, the promise of schooling is not. (2007- this may have changed since then)

There is a fee for entering the complex and parking; and parking is ample.

Getting there:
From Rapid City take Route # 16 south to the site, it will be on your left.

From Hot Springs take Route #16 /385 north to the site, it will be on the right.

Plan to spend:
The visit will take from two to four hours depending on what you want to see and how much shopping you want to do. There is a restaurant at the site and this will add an hour, if you partake of some goodies.

There is a separate fee for the bus ride that takes you to the base of the mountain where you can get a closer look.

12151 Ave of the Chiefs
Crazy Horse, SD 57730
43.828095, -103.631688

Hot Springs, South Dakota (Must See)

There are some advantages to staying in Hot Springs, and if you are planning to visit the *Mammoth Pits, Lakota Sioux Reservation, Wounded Knee, Custer State Park,* and *Mount Rushmore,* then it is a place to consider, but due to its small size the facilities can become scarce in the summer months, thus plan ahead, and make reservations well in advance.

Oglala Sioux Tribe Veterans Cemetery

Big Foot Trail, Kyle, SD 57752
43.450701, -102.024362

54

Pine Ridge Indian Reservation

This reservation is larger than the states of Delaware and Rhode Island combined and covers 3,468.86 square miles of South Dakota, it is the *eighth largest reservation* in the country.

{Chief Little Wound with his wife and son. (1899 Heyn photo) –Public Domain}

The problem is that it is also dirt poor and sparsely populated due to lack of infrastructure, roads, electricity, water, and waste disposal. Unemployment is about 89% (2005 was the last records we found) even though there is over $33,000,000 in revenue generated from the land use. Unfortunately, less than one third of this money gets to the members of the reservation as it is in corporate and other private hands.

Recently the tribe tried several business adventures, with limited to no success, until they opened the *Prairie Wind Casino* just outside Pine Ridge on Route #18. The tribe also operates the *White River*

Visitor Center near the *Badlands National Park* and it owns the *Lakota Country Times* newspaper and a radio station KILI-FM in the town of *Porcupine*.

The latest adventure is to generate electricity for sale via wind and solar generating plants, it remains to be seen if this will work as the major electric distribution systems are balking at letting the tribe sell electric to the grid networks.

In the Lakota language the name is *Oglala Oyanke*, and it is part of the *Oglala Sioux* Native American reservations.

If one wants to study the history of the reservation he or she should look up Wounded Knee, February 27, 1973; *Marlon Brando* and *Sacheen Littlefeather*; Murder capital of the US 1974; *Ray Robinson* and *Martin Luther King*; *Robert Robideau* and *Dino Butler* - June 26, 1975; *Leonard Peltier* 1975; *Anna Mae Aquash*, a *Mi'kmaq* *activist* - February 24, 1976; *Cecilia Fire Thunder* - March 21, 2006;

Crazy Horse; *Chief Red Cloud*; *Chief Touch the Clouds*; *Chief Big Foot*; *SuAnne Big Crow*; *Russell Means*; *Barbara Coe*; *Billy Mills* who won the gold medal at the 1964 Olympic Games; and *JoAnn Tall*

Getting there:
From Rapid City take Route #44 east to Scenic and then veer south through the Badlands. From *Hot Springs*, South Dakota, take Route #385 south to Route #18 east. Travel on route #18 east to *Pine Ridge.*

Plan to spend:
The drive from Rapid City and back will take the good part of a day, and you should plan to visit the *Badlands National Park* and the *Wounded Knee Memorial* during your ride.

From Hot Springs the drive is about an hour. If you stop in the casino, plan to spend time having a meal and doing some gaming.

Red Cloud Indian School

This is a school and *Heritage Center museum* run by the Lakota people of the *Pine Ridge Reservation*. It is located just outside Pine Ridge on Route # 18.

From their website:

"The Heritage Center of Red Cloud Indian School opened as a museum in 1982. It offers to the public - local, national, and international - an outstanding collection of Native American fine arts and Lakota tribal arts, located on the main campus of Red Cloud Indian School."

"One of the early successful museums located on an Indian reservation, The Heritage Center's fine arts collection includes over two thousand paintings, drawings, and sculptures representing a large number of different Native American tribal

traditions. Its tribal arts collection concentrates on traditional Lakota arts and history. "

"The Heritage Center serves as an extremely valuable cultural resource not only for the students of Red Cloud Indian School but for students of the other reservation schools and for all the Lakota people of the Pine Ridge Indian Reservation."

Annual Red Cloud Indian Art Show

"Our annual Art Show exhibits the exciting work of artists from tribes throughout the United States and Canada. The Art Show is open to the public and can be visited 7 days a week; admission is free. During the Art Show, free tours are available to the public."

Mission Statement

"The mission of The Heritage Center is to collect, preserve and exhibit the fine arts and tribal arts of Native Americans. We will concentrate on the fine arts of all Native Americans and the tribal arts of the Lakota. We will promote the arts of Native Americans to bring a greater appreciation of their culture. "

Admission may be free, suggested minimum donations to support our mission are welcome.

Wounded Knee Graveyard / Monument (Must See)

This small hilltop cemetery sits out on the plains near the town of Pine Ridge, South Dakota.

There is a small parking lot where you can park and then walk to the gravesites. The day we were there, a church group from the East Coast had just pulled up and was having a prayer service; this made for an emotionally filled morning as the tears flooded upon the soil that contained the souls and blood of so many Native Americans.

Getting there:

From *Hot Springs*, South Dakota, take Route #385 south to Route #18 east. Travel on route #18 east past *Pine Ridge* until you see a road that heads north on your left. The intersection is poorly marked, and you have to turn on faith, but it will take you directly to a hilltop that overlooks a valley, a small stream, and a small village. As you proceed down into  the valley you will see a small hill with a brown building at its top; the building will be surrounded by gravestones, and a taller memorial that is surrounded by a chain link fence, that is Wounded Knee the site of one of the worse USA disasters in recent history.

(Pictures, top is the graveyard and church, middle is a church group that held services there. They were from the mid-west; bottom is the interior of the native run museum.)

Plan to spend:

If you are there by yourself, plan to spend about 30 to 50 minutes at the graves, and about 30 minutes at the small museum at the foot of the hill.

The trip from *Hot Springs* will take about 5 hours roundtrip, so do the one way tour, and visit the *Badlands National Park, Wall Drugs,* the *Native American Museum,* and the *Native American Casino,* thus making it a long but fruitful day.

History of Wounded Knee

The AIM or *American Indian Movement* and the *Lakota tribe* for years had problems with the BLM, *Bureau of Land Management* and the FBI, *Federal Bureau of Investigation* over the appointed leadership of the tribe, this disagreement came to a head on the 28th of February, 1973 and the Federal Government sent in the troops for a 71 day standoff, which resulted in the killings of two warriors.

The older history is tragic to say the least, the U.S. Government in December 29, 1890, massacred almost 300 *Lakota Sioux* men, women, and children at what would become known as the *Wounded Knee Massacre.*

Chief Bigfoot and his followers were trying to get to *Pine Ridge* when intercepted by the 7th Cavalry.

Wounded Knee, SD 57794
43.142282, -102.364872

Wounded Knee Graveyard Site

Since I was there they have built a parking area and memorial along the highway. Not sure if you can still drive up the hill and park next to the church and graveyard. Do so if allowed, it is an emotional experience.

US-18
Pine Ridge, SD 57770
43.046514, -102.377169

Wounded Knee Museum

At the foot of the hill is a small round building that is the Native American Wounded Knee Museum, there is no charge for entry (2010), but a donation of a dollar or two is more than welcomed.

Be careful, sometimes there will be 'scalpers' outside at the door who will be pretending to be collecting for the museum, the donation jar is 'inside' the door.

There is another museum located at Exit 110 on Interstate 90 in Wall, South Dakota; the pictures here are from the museum at the hillside gravesite. (2010)

The museum has some Native American artifacts, but is mostly a visual history of the people of Wounded Knee and their disagreement with the United States of America, as shown in a surround of hand-painted murals.

Shown is a painting of *Chief Fire Lightning*.

Chapter # 09 – Utah:

The following text and pictures are from the author's book.

A Guide to Utah's National Parks
&
Great Attractions

William (Bill) C. McElroy
Copyright November 9, 2018
ISBN 9798713573652

Anasazi State Park Museum

Anasazi State Park Museum provides a look at 1,400-year-old ancestral Native American ruins. There is a small museum and gift shop on this site just south of Capitol Reef National Park on UT-12. Plan on one to two hours.

Anasazi State Park Museum
460 UT-12, Boulder, UT 84716
37.910932, -111.423482

Bloomington Petroglyph Park

Neighborhood park with several large boulders that have Petroglyph drawings on each. May or may not be genuine as it is not a very secure location and some of the 'scratchings' may be done by visitors. Plan on 30 minutes.

Bloomington Petroglyph Park
1460 W Navajo Drive,
St. George, UT 84790
37.052629, -113.615526

Canyonlands National Park

This national park is near Arches National Park and will take from a few hours to a day to explore. There are two (2) entry roads, one south of Moab and one at Moab. The Needles entry will provide you with views of Petroglyphs at Newspaper Rock, small ponds in solid rock that have life, and a cave-like ancient camping site with a hiking trail.

The north entry is the main entry that will take you to the Dead Horse Point State Park and to the Island in the Sky Visitor's Center. You will also see the Orange Cliffs Overlook and the Grand View Point overlook. There are camping areas, and lots to see. Plan on six to eight hours.

Canyonlands National Park
112 UT-313
Moab, UT 84532
38.672484, -109.686508

Fort Bluff

Almost drove by this interesting reconstruction of the fort and old town.

This is a great stop on the way to Arches or Canyonlands from the south side of Utah. Great guides, clean restrooms, good ice cream, and lots to see and learn about the pioneers, Native Americans, and others that settled here.   There are around twenty (20) 1880 era reconstructed buildings to view, so plan on spending from two to four hours minimum.

Bluff Fort
550 East Black Locust
Bluff, UT 84512

Fremont Indian State Park and Museum

This Utah State Park features Native American Petroglyphs &
Pictographs, and an 800 to 1,000 foot walkway to the cliffs and
caves that contain many. Plan on one to two hours.

Fremont Indian S.P. and Museum
3820 Clear Creek Canyon Road,
Sevier, UT 84766
38.576185,-112.34971

Frontier Homestead State Park Museum

(Formerly Iron Mission State Park)
This park has several reconstructed buildings and features sleighs,
stagecoaches, and vintage vehicles.   There are several Native
American dwelling replicas and an iron blast furnace replica. Plan
on one to three hours and try to stay out of their Jail.

Frontier Homestead State Park Museum
635 N. Main
Cedar City, UT 84721
37.688439,-113.062878

Hovenweep National Monument

This national monument has ancient native Indian ruins on the
hillside, the Hovenweep Castle, and in the valley just below the
castle. There are camping grounds at the site. Plan on two to four
hours.

Hovenweep Castle
Montezuma Creek, UT 84534
37.385888, -109.080534

Hovenweep Visitor Center
Montezuma Creek, UT 84534
37.385815, -109.075388

Josie Morris Cabin

Part of Dinosaur National Park, this is a historic cabin on a beautiful picnic site with a restroom. This area has Petroglyphs within an easy walk, and there are trails to Box and Hog Canyons. Plan on 15 to 25 minutes.

Jensen, UT 84035
40.425436, -109.174836

Newspaper Rock State Historical Monument

See Canyonlands National Park as this is on the south entry road, UT-211. There are many Petroglyphs on the side of the hill on the side of the road, and thus you can spend 5 to 10 minutes in wonder, or days if you try to figure out what was being said at the time these scratchings were created. Since I was there, there appears to be better parking and a restroom for your convenience. You are 22 miles from the main section of the park.

Newspaper Rock State Historical Monument
UT-211, Monticello, UT 84535
37.988462, -109.518176

Peteetneet Academy and Museum

This 1897 building and grounds house a school, playground, and museum all in one; it is named after Indian Chief Peteetneet who helped the pioneers of his day get settled in the area. Plan on one hour.

Peteetneet Academy & Museum
10 N 600 E, Payson, UT 84651
40.043604, -111.724066

Ripple Rock Nature Center

This is one of the attractions at Capitol Reef National Park

Per the NPS website

"The nature center helps to educate youth and enhance their understanding of American Indian culture, pioneer history, geology, paleontology, astronomy, wildlife, and much more. The goal of the nature center is not to simply teach park visitors about the many wonders within the park, but to foster curiosity through playful activities. Ripple Rock Nature Center programs and displays target family groups, but there is something fun for everyone to enjoy."

Plan on one to two hours.

Ripple Rock Nature Center
281 Scenic Drive,
Torrey, UT 84775
38.286965, -111.248714

Uintah County Heritage Museum

From Official website

"Uintah County Heritage Museum features displays of the pioneers, Native American Indians, miners, soldiers, lawmen and outlaws who helped shape the history of the Uinta Basin"

Plan on one to two hours.

Uintah County Heritage Museum
155 E Main Street,
Vernal, UT 84078
40.456060, -109.525360

Chapter # 10 – Wyoming:

The following text and pictures are from the author's book.

Wyoming's Must See Attractions!

By William C. McElroy

Copyright

© Copyright 2010-2018 by William C. McElroy, DBA User Friendly Operational Software, all rights reserved.

ISBN: 9798713451943

Ayres Natural Bridge Park

Do you dare to go to this tourist attraction? There is an evil spirit that lives under the rock formation that is one of the only three in the US that spans flowing water. It seems that when Native Americans lived there, a bolt of lightning struck a young brave that was hunting in the canyon and this then became a place not to be as the spirit (lightning god?) would strike you too dead

Battle of Tongue River

This battle was a success and a failure all in one. Jim Bridger and

Brigadier General Patrick Edward Connor were assigned to stop the Indian raids on the Bozeman trail and those using it.
The August 1965 attack on Arapaho Indian tribe resulted in the killing of many women and children, and eventually led to days of battle and the attack on the Sawyers Expedition. The other more less known event was that due to the length of the battles the powder used for loading the guns became in limited supply, and thus the soldiers were forced to use 'short' loads that resulted in the bullets hitting and bouncing off the intended targets, the Indians, (i.e. Native Americans).

There is camping nearby, and at the Connor site.

Lazy R Campground
652 US-14, Ranchester, WY 82839
44.908226, -107.166954

Connor Battlefield Historic Site
55 US-14, Ranchester, WY 82839
44.905453, -107.162764

Bozeman Trail Museum

Back a few years ago, say in 1879, the Rock Creek Stage Line connected Virginia City, Montana with the southeastern sections of Wyoming along the Bozeman Trail. Travelers needed a place to get wagons fixed, horses shoed, and other items sharpened or repaired, and thus O.P. Hanna decided to build his home at the location; later in 1879 the Rock Creek Stage Line constructed a Blacksmith shop at the location.

The museum features blacksmith tools, artifacts from the gold seeking pioneers, books, clothing, dentistry equipment, Native American artifacts, and photos. The museum is open at certain days and months of the year, thus check their website for exact information.

There is ample parking, and the museum shares the lot with another building. The museum is hand-hewn from local lumber; the building and has been restored for your enjoyment.

Bozeman Trail Museum
Johnson Street,
Big Horn, WY 82833
44.679493, -106.991349

Carbon County Museum

This local museum may be free to enter, but it is not lacking in full size displays of the Union Pacific Railroad via a massive photomural and full size mannequins of railroad workers. There are also full size mockups of Native Americans and their living areas, and of a 1930's ranch. There is an old fire engine and a sheep wagon, along with some old mining equipment for your enjoyment.

One items stands out, that is a pair of shoes made from the skin of the notorious Big Nose George, i.e., George Francis Warden, a.k.a. George Parrot, a.k.a. "Big Nose George" a notorious 1870's cattle rustler and train robber.

Carbon County Museum,
904 W Walnut Street
Rawlins, WY 82301
41.790952, -107.247106

Clusters Expedition

This is a roadside marker that provides some history of the area and the interaction between the settlers and the Native Americans.

Do not have a GPS for this roadside marker, sorry. If you have the GPS for this, then place it in the Amazon Kindle comments for this book. Thanks.

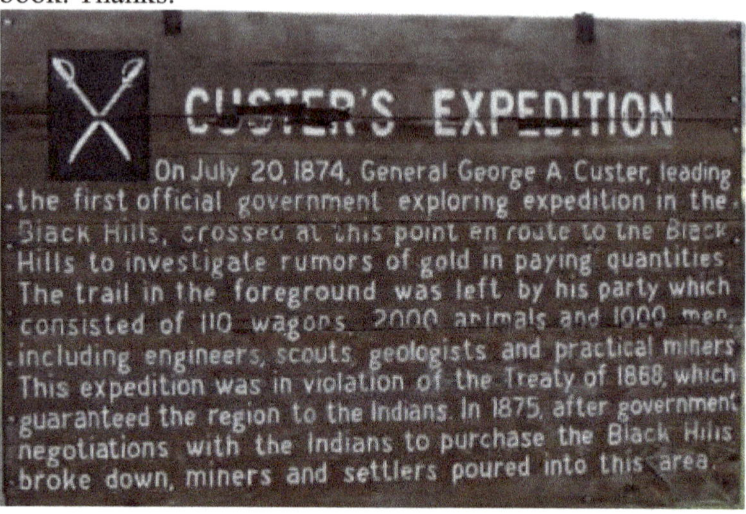

Colter Bay Indian Museum

This is a very sad National Park location as it is NOW PERMANENTLY CLOSED {Oct 2018}

Colter Bay Visitor Center {Closed}
Moran, WY 83013
43.903225, -110.643617

Fetterman Monument

"Give me 80 men and I can ride thought the Sioux Nation" a quote
from Captain Fetterman just before being soundly defeated by the
Sioux and Crazy Horse in December of 1866.

Fetterman Monument
Banner, WY 82832
44.570777, -106.839617

South entry from I-90 and US-87
Piney Creek Road
Banner, WY 82832
44.539839, -106.821862

North entry from I-90 and US-87
Piney Creek Road
Banner, WY 82832
44.600947, -106.866120

First National Bank Museum

This is not the museum in Pennsylvania of the same name. The
town of Meeteetse has several museums and if you care to take a
day or two some tours to a western ranch, a ghost town, the location
of ~300 pieces of Dinwoody rock art (Petroglyphs), and the
unfinished foundation of Amelia Earhart's summer residence (She
went missing over the Pacific before it was finished).

First National Bank Museum
1033 Park Ave,
Meeteetse, WY 82433
44.156994, -108.872446

Fort Phil Kearny

We arrived here from Rapid City five minutes after closing and were
greeted by the caretaker that took pity on us and allowed us to enter
and take pictures.

Fort provides some history of the Sioux Indian Wars. Much of the fort was burned to the ground after the army abandoned it, and thus you will not see many buildings, only the outer fence and the foundations. There is though the main exhibit and lots of history to explore here. The personnel are friendly and knowledgeable about the fort and its history. Plan on 30 minutes to an hour or more at this location.

From Wikipedia website.

The Bozeman Trail.

"....the Sioux attacked the United States anyway, claiming that the Yellowstone was now their land". Indian raids along the trail and around the forts continued. When the Lakota annihilated a detachment under William J. Fetterman at the Fetterman Fight near Fort Phil Kearny on December 21, 1866, civilian travel along the trail ceased. On August 1, 1867, and August 2, 1867, U.S. forces resisted coordinated attempts by large parties of Lakota and Cheyenne to overrun Fort C. F. Smith and Fort Phil Kearny in the Hayfield Fight and Wagon Box Fight.

The Fetterman monument is not far from this location.

Fort Phil Kearny
528 Wagon Box Road
Banner, WY 82832
44.532298, -106.826547

Wagon Box Battle Monument

About 2 miles northwest of Fort Phil Kearny you will find this
monument to the brave that protected the woodcutters that were
working there.

Wagon box is so named for the inch thick wooden wagon beds
(boxes) removed from the supply wagons to build a coral for the
livestock and storage of supplies. The woodcutter's camp was
attacked by Chief Red Cloud's warriors on August 2, 1867 and was
holding its own until Major Benjamin Smith arrived with howitzers,
at which time the natives were outgunned and retreated. There are
placards at the site that tell the entire story. Worth the hours drive
and visit to see and learn this history.

Wagon Box Battle Monument
Story, WY 82832
44.558698, -106.903170

Wind River Indian Reservation

This is the home of the Eastern Shoshone and Northern Arapaho
Native American tribes.

Wind River Indian Reservation
Kinnear, WY 82516
43.300198, -108.839620

Chapter # 11 – Rules, Regulations, and Laws:

Archaeological Resource Protection Act (ARPA) of 1979

Mining and off-road vehicle use are now prohibited and the Archaeological Resource Protection Act (ARPA) of 1979 protects archaeological sites. ARPA provides for protection of archaeological resources on public and Native American lands. Penalties for ARPA violations can result in up to a year in jail and $100,000 in fines for misdemeanor convictions, and up to two years in jail and $250,000 in fines for felony convictions.

One may do off-road driving in the National Parks on the marked roads and trails. You need to get permission at the Visitors Center of each park, and there may be an added park entry fee for this.

Use common sense when passing another vehicle on the roads, and be aware that the high speed limits, 65 to 75 MPH (Miles per Hour) will require great distances to pass safely, and that you may have to accelerate to speeds of 90 or 100 MPH during a passing maneuver.

The roads are well marked as to when and where you may pass, and in some instances the roads are built especially for passing. Route 264, which crosses the *Navajo and Hopi reservations*, has three lanes, one for eastbound traffic, one for westbound traffic, and a center lane for passing. The passing is done in alternate strips of road where there will be no passing for west bound traffic for a mile or two, then no passing for eastbound traffic or a mile or two, then back to no passing for west bound, and then eastbound. This apparently works and saved the state money in that only three, not four lanes were needed.

Chapter 19 - Driving in the American Southwest

Driver's Licenses

You may not require a driver's license if all transportation is provided with a purchased tour, thus it should be left at home or locked up in a secure place. If you lose a wallet it should be devoid of as much identification, cash, and credit cards as possible.

The exception is if you are traveling over the International border to and from Mexico, in which case you will need to show your driver's license, and maybe a birth certificate, passport, or other approved ID.

Southwest USA Tourist Information - Driver's Licenses

If you do desire to rent a vehicle then you may be required to have a proper driver's license and proper *State required insurance*. Note that you will be asked for a credit card or a cash deposit when renting a vehicle. Most national *car rental companies* will not take cash if you are renting within the state where your driver's license is issued, and therefore you must use a *credit card*. You may though be able to use a cash deposit in states where you are not licensed, but you should check ahead for the rules.

The speed limits on all highways are posted and the police do monitor the traffic, but due to the expanses of the area, the police are few and far between. Highway speed limits are posted at 55 to 75 MPH depending on the congestion of the area; speeds of 80+ are common so be prepared for high speed driving.

Speed limits through towns are in the 25 to 40 MPH range and are well posted; small towns finance their police departments with ease, so be forewarned. School zones during school hours usually have a speed limit of 15 MPH, strictly enforced.

Planning is everything, and getting to or from an airport can be interesting. Most airports are built on the outskirts of a town or city and therewithal are a problem as most urban sprawl housing is built on the outskirts of a town or city. During rush hours the local highways and Interstates may be clogged with those commuters trying to get to work or home; and you should give yourself extra time if your flight is scheduled during those hours, or if you have to pick up or return a rental vehicle at the airport. The same applies to the downtown areas of a town or city; the commuters may have traffic clogged for hours.

Note that if you are taking the railroads or bus to a town or city and then renting a vehicle, the vehicle rentals are generally at the airport and thus, you have to plan for the transportation from and to the airport from the rail or bus station.

The distance between the National Parks on the Great Circle are considerable and therefore, one can easily find oneself sleeping or hypnotized by the straight, sometimes boring roads. Additionally, long-term sitting can affect blood flow to the legs and feet and cause health problems, therefore it is advisable to make a stop every hour or so and spend a few minutes walking and taking in the grander of the area's scenery. There are view areas and some rest stops on most of the Interstate highways, and some of the local and state operated roads; this includes roadside placards that describe the area and its attributes.

One must get use to the fact that he or she is in control of his or her vehicle at all times and the various authorities are not your body guards, i.e., there are frequently NO guardrails in areas where one would expect to find a guardrail. Thus, if the posted speed is fifteen miles per hour around a mountain curve, then it is highly recommended that you comply with the posted speed. When climbing or descending mountain curves it is recommended that you shift to a lower gear in order to maintain power and control over your vehicle.

The Great Circle route consists of several State, local, and Federal highways. The travel on these roads is not bad and most are well maintained in the three non-winter seasons. In the dead of winter, the story may change as there is snow in the area and the many miles of roads can take considerable time to be cleared. I-70 is one such road, as if you are coming from *Denver*, it has to climb up and over the *Rocky Mountains* at an elevation of over 10,000 feet. You may also find that many of the National Park roads are closed for periods during the winter months; these roads are usually two lane, long, winding, and hilly. The author has even experienced snow closures in June at Crater Lake in Oregon and in October on the north rim of the Grand Canyon.

Chapter # 12 – Safety:

Medical concerns:

Make sure to take any medications that you require and let your guide know of any 'specific' medical problems that may affect or effect your comfort and safety during the ride, especially if doing an overnight or multi-day ride.

Medical Facilities

Oxygen Levels - Oxygen Starvation

The *altitude* of most of the Great Circle is above 5,280 feet above sea level and there will be many times that one is at the 8,000 and even 9,000 plus foot levels (*Shown is Rainbow Point at Bryce Canyon* 

National Park elevation 9,115 feet above sea level) where the air is thin and it becomes difficult for many to properly breathe.

One may feel that breathing is labored and that one is light-headed from lack of oxygen. Rest assured, the a healthy person will maintain proper *Blood to Oxygen ratio* (95 – 100% is normal) and his or her blood pressure and heart rate will be normal, if it was normal before the trip.

Many of the ERs (*Emergency Rooms*) at the local hospitals will give you a complementary or low cost check-up, if you are uncomfortable and feel that you may have serious problems.

When Traveling our nation one may have a traffic accident, or a medical emergency, or some other on-the-road problem, and knowing who to call can mean the difference between life or death. So, one of our readers came across the following website and suggested we include it here. The site includes the names, addresses, and phone numbers of local police and emergency services from State to State, town to town. While we know that 911 can be fast, it may be faster and easier to contact local authorities, so here is the link

{Note: We are not responsible for their information}

Additionally, road, accident, and weather conditions can cause delays and closures, so each state has a website that you can access for the latest information. Contact the nearest AAA facility for their Highway Conditions Maps and charts for your intended trip. {Note: We are not responsible for their information}

Hospitals in the Southwestern U.S.A. - Visitor's Guide

One of the things many people forget about when traveling is that he or she may need the services of a medical facility, for sickness, accidents, or for change of altitude breathing problems. Thus, you should chart out any facilities that you might need, before you take your trip.

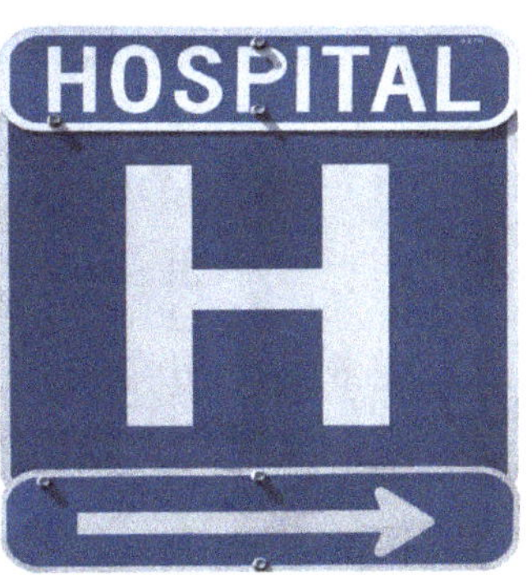

Weather

The west and southwest are both desert and mountainous, and the weather is fickle. It is usually cool to freezing at night, and warm to boiling during the day. There is a rainy season called a Monsoon, and a dry creek or valley can become a flood zone in seconds, even if the rain is a hundred miles distant. Check the weather forecast before traveling.

Chapter # 13 – Road Closures:

December to April the following roads are closed to normal traffic due to heavy snow. Verify that the roads are open in November and May as there can be early or late snow that temporarily blocks access.

US-16 / US-20 {Closed in winter}
Yellowstone National Park, WY 82190
44.474020, -110.054985

Grand Loop Road / US-191 - Tower Junction {Closed in winter}
Yellowstone National Park, WY 82190
44.915966, -110.415783

Norris Canyon Road, {Closed in winter}
Yellowstone National Park, WY 82190
44.735968, -110.493853

West Entry Road, {Closed in winter}
US-191 / US-287 / US-20
Yellowstone National Park, WY 82190
44.651193, -111.030702

When one travels he or she can find himself or herself in medical trouble, be it getting food poisoning, a vehicle accident, a sickness, or a fall, etc., and therefore, it is helpful to know in advance that there is medical help and facilities in the area of which he or she is touring. Here is a short-listing of some of the major medical centers that you should know. Yes, there is 911, but you will be in remote areas and may be out of reach of our cell phone reception regions.

GPS Use & Helpful tips

Designing your trip using the GPS number location provide in this manual

Map & Direction Information

The maps & directions provided are well researched and assumed accurate; but are dependent on third party sources that this author has little to no control over, thus you MUST Verify all directions and GPS coordinates to your satisfactions, this author is NOT Responsible for your or others actions in the use of the information provided.

Avoiding GPS Problems

When a person enters a GPS coordinate, the computers will plot out a path for the user from and to destinations, which is all well and good, except that many times the roads or turns are NOT suitable for RVs, trucks, busses, certain types of drivers; and many times the roads are blocked or otherwise not accessible. The author of this e-book did a map and picture search of questionable intersections and had avoided these locations as best possible; while suggesting better roads that lead you right into the nearest parking lot of the place you are visiting.

Using GPS - Major Highways

Many GPS coordinates start you at some road or remote place that you have absolutely no idea of, or where each is; the GPS provided on this e-book takes you from the nearest major State or US Interstate Highway Exit turn-by-turn to your intended destination.

No GPS in your Vehicle

Lots of people do NOT have GPS in their vehicles and therefore, the GPS coordinates may seem to be useless; this is not true as since you are reading this, you have a computer. Thus, you can view the GPS and the roads and turn-by-turn

paths to your destination and draw or plot out the Road &
Town Names and the distances so that you can take your
created maps with you.

GPS Coordinate Numbers

Some mapping programs will allow you to enter the GPS
numbers and the program will not only provide a picture
map of the places, but also a point to point set of instructions.
For example:

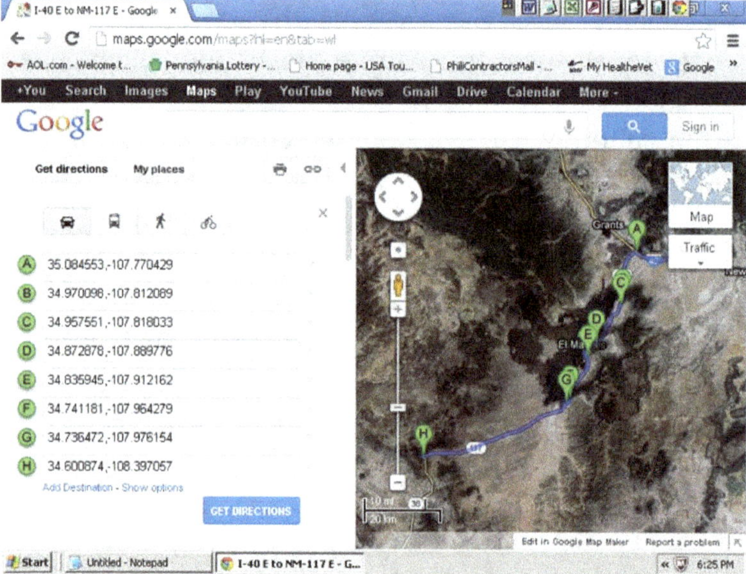

1. Head **southeast** on **I-40 E**
2. Take exit **96** toward **McCartys/Acoma/Sky City**
3. Turn left onto **State Rd 124**
4. Turn right to merge onto **I-40 W**
5. Take exit **89** toward **Quemado**

This allows you to print out your map book with full
directions and if using some programs the distances and time
to budget.

Red Instructions on Pages

Many of the locations have restrictions or are subject to
weather, flooding, closures, etc., many GPS direction sites do
NOT provide 'Cautions' or 'Warnings' that can get you into
major trouble or at a minimum result in you missing out on
some fabulous site that you wanted to see.

This manual, although not perfect in catching all, all the time,
has done its best to find these 'problem areas' and NOTE each
so that you arrive safely at your intended destination. We
advise our readers to consult those links (State and Federal
websites) to see the most UP-to-DATE Information and
Warnings.

No-GPS Provided

Many of the sites in the Southwest are on Private Property or
Native American Reservations and therefore, you MUST
contact the owners or authorities for permissions and for
specific directions, and for dates and times you may view the
sites. Some sites are *Archaeological sites* that are restricted to
those that sign up for a 'dig' or 'educational' tour. Contact the
respective websites for information, the link(s) to these are
provided on each page.

No-GPS in Remote Areas

When traveling using some GPS systems the system uses local
microwave towers for transmission of the GPS information
and thus, mountains, distance, valleys, etc., can interrupt
these transmissions, and you may find yourself out in the
wilderness without GPS or Cell Phone communication. Thus,
let people know where you may be on any specific day, and
take maps with you or have the entire route plotted out on
paper, before you leave.

Advertised GPS vs. this book's GPS Coordinates

We use Wikipedia, State, Local, National Park Service, and other 'official' type websites to find information for our destination pages, and many of these post GPS coordinates that will get you within feet to miles of the actual place you can visit. This is true of National Forest GPS that usually puts you in the center of the forest, but not anywhere near to a road or the park's visitor's center.

This manual's GPS tries to get you to within feet of the *Parking Lot entry* where you will be visiting; the actual site or specific building is near. Where it is known, I also post the parking lot entry requirement for RVs, Busses, trucks, and automobiles.

GPS for Highway Intersections

Interstate Exits can cover considerable distances from where you leave the highway to where the cross road actually crosses. This site provides Interstate name, the Exit number, and the GPS coordinate of the 'X' where the roads cross. You need to know that your turn-off can be anywhere from feet to a half-mile of the 'X', and adjust accordingly.

Chapter # 14 – Suggested Itinerary:

Creating an itinerary presents a challenge to a traveler in that he or she may be interested in different aspects of the Native American culture, or in the starting or ending points of their trip to the American West and Southwest, or how much time he or she has for seeing all that can be seen, or the amount of money he or she has allocated for the trip.

So, let's zero in on what you are seeking.

State – AZ, CA, CO, NM, NV, SD, UT, WY (Select as desired)

Main City for Arrival to the US SW – Phoenix, Tucson, Las Angeles, Denver, Albuquerque, Las Vegas, Rapid City, Salt Lake, Jackson Hole (Select as desired)

Transportation – Public Bus, Public Train, Regional Air, Private Bus, Rental Vehicle, Touring Van (Select as desired)

Days Available – One through XXX – (Enter # of Days)

What to See – Ancient Ruins, Reservations, Casinos, Museums, State Parks, National Parks, Shopping Areas, Artwork, Reconstructed Villages, Native Dances & Pow Wows (Select as desired)

Accommodations – On a Native American Reservation, in a Campground, or in a RV Camp, Motel, Hotel, Tent, with Friends, with Relatives, Bed & Breakfast, Hostel, Apartment, Resort (Select as desired)

Food & Drink – Near Hotel, In the Hotel, Native American Food, Ethnic Food, Alcohol Required, Cost Range, Meals per Day, Dietary Restrictions (Select as desired)

Activates – Walking tours, Van tours, Bus tours, Horseback Riding, Boating, Train Ride, Air or Balloon Ride, Helicopter Ride, Whitewater Rafting, Archeological Dig, Jeep Ride, River Boat Ride,

Dancing, Gambling, Cooking Lessons, Mountain Climbing, Hiking, Cave Exploring, Biking, Visiting Museums (Select as desired)

Dollar Amount per Day per Person – **$xxx.xx** (Enter # of Dollars)

Main City for Departure from the US SW – Phoenix, Tucson, Las Angeles, Denver, Albuquerque, Las Vegas, Rapid City, Salt Lake, Jackson Hole (Select as desired)

RECOMMENDATIONS:

State – Arizona and New Mexico are highly populated with Native American ruins, reservations, museums, and activities like Pow Wows and casinos.

Main City for Arrival to the US SW – If entering from Las Angeles (LAX) or New York (JFK) the better cities are Las Vegas (LAS) Phoenix (PHX), Albuquerque (ABQ), and Denver (DEN)

Tucson (TUC) is good if you are going to the southern Arizona towns and attractions of Benson, Bisbee, Chiricahua, Fairbank, Fort Bowie, Douglas, Dragoon, Naco, Tombstone, Sierra Vista and Willcox. Rent a car and plan on a two to three day stay at the minimum. Best time of year is late winter and early spring as there are lots of events. Summer is very hot, over 100 degrees F.

Transportation – A rental vehicle should be the first choice as there are few if any transportation options to many or most of the sites you might want to visit. There are tours by bus or private van, but these require having set attractions and regimented travel; and each can be costly and involved being with from 12 to 45 other travelers.

Days Available – At a minimum you should consider three days, but to see just the main highlights, it will take about 15 days. Figure seeing one to three closely positioned sites per day. Many travelers would consider two events per day as the maximum.

What to See – A ruin is a ruin, a museum is a museum, and a casino is a casino. The trick to enjoying your western and southwest trip is to mix it up with one or two of each attraction, and perhaps some others that are NOT considered Native American.

Accommodations – This is up to you and yours, but if you are going to need any of the listed accommodations, then you need to 'reserve' your spot three or more months in advance. You also need to understand that if you are on the Internet and you look up a place to stay, do not look at it 'over and over again'. Companies see this and in many instances will keep raising the price, as they know you want to stay in their facility.

Food & Drink – There are McDonalds and Burger Kings along with just about every other fast-food place you can think of in the major US cities. Some cities in the southwest like Tucson have an abundance of Mexican cuisine. Some of the hotels and motels have free breakfast, and some have full-fledged restaurants. Try to seek out a quality restaurant for dinner that is within a mile or so of your overnight accommodations and map it out so you don't get lost. (It is easy to get lost in a town or city you have not been it before)

CAUTION: Alcoholic beverages are NOT allowed to be taken on or served on any of the Native American Reservations.

CAUTION: Water can vary considerably from location to location, and thus using bottled water may be a necessity.

Budget at a minimum some $45 to $60 per day per person for meals. Note that you may not be eating too many lunches while on the road, or at many of the attractions due to lack of places to eat.

Activities – Museums can be free in some areas, most charge under $10 USD (United States Dollars) for entry. Tours can range from about $40 to into the thousands. Balloon, Jeep, Rafting, and other rides will cost from $100 USD to well over $500 USD.

Archeological Digs are by invitation and you must comply with the laws and the administrator's request. Schedule your dig a year in advance and expect to work, get your hands dirty, spend time sleeping in the wild, and spending several thousand USD.

Dollar Amount per Day per Person – Figure that you will need food ($60), accommodations ($55), rental vehicle ($35), gasoline and tolls ($15), entry fees ($15), and extras ($15) per day per person. That comes to $195 PP or $390 USD for two. Thus a typical 8-day trip, not counting airfare for two will cost about $3,120.00.

Main City for Departure from the US SW – Your best bet is to make your trip circular so you leave from the same airport in which you arrived. To leave at a different airport may cost more for the airline ticket and for the vehicle rental.

Rental Vehicles
Take pictures of the vehicle before you leave the rental lot, and be sure to note the condition, the gasoline level, and any other problems with the vehicle. Upon return to the rental company be sure to again take pictures and fill the tank back to the original level.

Note that if you drop the vehicle off at a different rental location from where you picked it up, you may have to pay to have it returned to the original location.

Also note, that if you get a traffic or parking ticket you are responsible and that you may not know about the ticket until weeks later when you return home and receive a notice in the mail.

Disease and Allergies
The American Southwest has all sorts of pollen producing plants and therefore if you are sensitive to allergies, be sure to bring or purchase medication for it.

There is also the matter of sunburn and sunstroke, so wear sunscreen and a hat. Long sleeve shirts and leg covering is recommended.

Do not go digging in the dirt as it may contain the mold that can cause Valley Fever a respiratory disease.

If hiking in the mountains, stay on the trails and watch for rattlesnakes, they do not always give warning.

Appendix I – Glossary of Terms:

Anasazi / Ancestral Puebloan – These are the peoples that settled the areas and built many of the ruins that you may visit today.

Bureau of Indian Affairs (BIA) – This is a U.S. Government agency that 'helps' the Native Americans during disputes and other legal affairs

Bureau of Indian Education (BIE) – This is a U.S. Government agency that 'helps' the Native Americans become properly educated.

BLM – Bureau of Land Management. This is a U.S. Governmental agency that has control over land use and in many instances the lands or reservations owned by the Native American Communities. It is the source of the BLM 1780 Tribal Relations Manual.

Burial Ground – A sacred area of land that is used as a cemetery.

Casino – A building on a Native American land that contains a place for gambling. It may contain a bar, a restaurant, a show room, and a motet or hotel as well as gaming tables and slot machines.

Cliff House – A dwelling that is carved into a cliff or is under a cliff overhang. This is for protection from the elements and from one's enemies. May have several floors, each accessible by ladders.

Diné – These were the ancestors of the current Navajo and the Navajos still consider themselves to be members of the Diné communities. Diné translates to 'People'.

Division of Forestry (DOF) – This is a U.S. Government agency that 'helps' the Native American citizens to protect their forest and to understand how to utilize the natural resource of each.

Dream Catcher – This is a loop with hanging decorations that is designed to 'catch and trap' bad dreams, i.e. nightmares so that you get a good night's sleep. You hang these near your bed, or the entries to your home.

Four-Corners – This is the point where Utah, Colorado, New Mexico, and Arizona all meet. There is an in-ground plaque that you can stand on and have your picture taken, and there are restrooms, and plenty of Native American sales booths selling trinkets and other novelties.

Fry Bread – This is a Native American flatbread that is made from simple ingredients and then deep fried in lard or cooking oil. It may be sprinkled with powdered sugar or used as a base for other ingredients.

Headdress – A ceremonial head covering that may consist of feathers and other decorative elements.

Hogan – This is a small circular or six-sided, above ground home made from mud and straw brick and other native materials. Most are vacated today in lieu of more modern living quarters.

Hopi – This is a Native American tribe that is located in the middle of the Navajo nation. These citizens can be traced back to have come from Mexico in 500 B.C. and to have eventually settled in Oraibi, Awatovi, Wupatki, Betatakin, and the villages in Canyon De Chelly. They believe in Animism, a means of healing, bringing rain, and healing. They are the people that carve the Kachinas you will see for sale throughout the four-corners area.

Indian Affairs Manual (IAM) – This is a U.S. Government manual that consists of pages of instructions, laws, rules regulations, etc. that tribes are required to follow. The following link will provide you with the full content of this manual.

https://www.bia.gov/policy-forms/manual#view-field-chapter-table-column--54

Kachinas – These are small carved figures of animals and people that are considered by the Hopi as being or bringing good fortune, health, rain, food, and much more. Kachinas are somewhat collectable and many tourist purchase one or more.

Kiva – This is a circular, in-ground, domed meeting place for the 'men' to relax and talk about problems, futures, hunting, protecting their village, etc. It is considered off-limits to the women and it may be considered as a religious place for praying.

Medicine Man – A tribal elder that is permitted to cure one of his or her physical or mental ailments using prayer, song, smoke, herbs, and other means.

National Park Service (NPS) – This is a U.S. Government agency that runs the national park system in the United States of America. They are one of the primary organizations that oversee ancient Native American ruins. U.S. Senior Citizens can obtain park passes that allow him or her to enter most at minimum or no charge.

Navajo – This is the primary Native American tribe that lives in the American Southwestern states of Arizona and New Mexico. The word Navajo translates to 'farm fields in the valley' in referring to the people that were more domesticated and using the land for farming and survival.

Navajo Code Talkers – These were Navajo citizens that the U.S. Government hired during the WWII battles in the South Pacific. They used the Navajo Language to send over 800 messages that could not be deciphered by the Japanese, thus they helped save lives and win the war.

Office of Trust Services (OTS) – This is a U.S. Government agency that protects the 'trust' agreements made between authorities and tribes in relation to land holdings and use.

Peace Pipe – A specially designed smoking pipe used in ceremonies and other events. Passing the pipe to your opponent or enemy and having him smoke it was a sign of peace or peaceful agreement.

Petroglyph – This was a means of communication used along trails. The natives scratched various figures into the desert varnish (or patina), the blackish covering on a rock. The removal of the patina resulted in a lighter colored surface that displayed the message.

Desert varnish is primarily composed of particles of clay along with oxides of iron and manganese.

Pictographs – These are paintings using natural materials for the pigments. Many caves and ancient buildings have been found that contain pictures (pictographs) that have helped to establish the history of those that painted the pictures.

Pit House – This is a building technique in which a pit or dug out area is created and then post are used to create a structure with roofing. Pit houses were efficient in that being mostly under ground level each is somewhat immune to earthquakes, weather, and temperature changes. Living quarters included a fire pit, food storage area, living room, and bedding space.

Pow Wow – A yearly or more gathering of Native American citizens in which they dress in traditional costumes and perform various dances and other ceremonious activities.

Pueblo – This is a building or group of buildings that are the homes of many Native American citizens. It is also the term given to a group of homes and businesses that are a town.

Pueblo Peoples – Name given to those that live in Pueblos

Rain Stick – The Native American ceremony used to produce rain needed something that sounded like rain falling. The answer is to use a hollow rod and fill it with pebbles or seeds and then seal the ends. When shaken it makes the required rain falling sound.

Reservation – A plot of land set aside by the United States Government for the natives of America.

Sand Painting – Using mineral and plant dyed sand the artist or the medicine man places the sand in a frame to make a symmetrical picture. This sand painting is used in healing a person's physical or mental medical condition and it is both ceremonial and spiritual.

Teepee – A home (they dwell in) made from branches and covered with hide. It is a circular pyramid looking structure with a hole at the top for the elimination of cooking and heating fumes and smoke.

Waterway Ceremony – A Native ceremony designed to bring rain to the people, their animals, and their crops.

Window Rock – An arch or hole in a rock formation that to the natives may be considered a window into the future or to heaven. Window Rock is the capital of the Navajo Nation and the sandstone arch located there is sacred to the citizens. It is said that there once was a pool or water by the arch and the water was used for the Waterway Ceremony.

Appendix II – Native American Ruins - Directions to:

The following text and pictures are from the author's book.

RoadSites© tm
In the American Southwest
Southwestern Road Trips Colorado Version

By
William C. McElroy

Copyright 2016-2018

RoadSites© tm is a point a to point b guide that takes you along a road or highway and presents the various sites and sights that may be of interest to the driver and his or her passengers. The series of four includes Arizona, Colorado, New Mexico, and Utah.

Directions are provided from the nearest major town to the site's entry points, using best possible roads.

There may be other entry points on other roads, but many are remote and not paved, thus requiring something other than the family car.

Picture, prayer service at the *Wounded Knee Reservation Grave Site.*

Albuquerque, New Mexico
Petroglyph National Monument, Location: *Visitor center* is located 3 miles north of I-40 on Unser Boulevard. The Visitor Center is at

GPS 35.138388,-106.71087. Also go to GPS 35.167231,-106.724753 for the second section of the park, called *Boca Negra Canyon Trails*

Aztec, New Mexico
Aztec Ruins National Monument, Location: Outskirts of small northwestern New Mexico city of Aztec. GPS 36.834342,-108.000632

Chaco Culture National Historical Park, Location: N. Mex. 57 in northwestern New Mexico, 64 miles south of Aztec, N. Mex. GPS 36.028599,-107.904067 is the main in/out entry point, the entire complex is large and there is a one-way road the circles the main ruins that can be visited. Roads are a mix of pavement and dirt, check with NPS for details and local weather before making the long trip into the site.

Cortez, Colorado
Hovenweep National Monument, Location: 45 miles from Cortez, Colo., on Utah-Colorado border. GPS 37.383734,-109.072587, gets you to the park buildings and the Campground areas. Be prepared to do some walking, the ruins are in the canyons northwest of the parking area.

Flagstaff, Arizona
Grand Canyon South Rim Tusuyan Ruins at GPS 36.014541,-111.868892 is between the two ends of the south rim road. There is a museum and an old ancestral *Puebloan (Anasazi) ruins at Tusuyan Ruins.* Stop and spend some time, there are usually National Park Rangers there that give guided tours of the ruins with a verbal history of the peoples.   Parking lot is at GPS 36.013161,-111.866619.

Montezuma Castle is approximately 50 miles south of Flagstaff, Arizona and is off of I-17 at exit 298 just below McGuireville at GPS 34°36'47"N 111°50'24"W, the entry road is at GPS 34.604945,-111.858411 just opposite of the *Yavapai Complex and Cliff Castle Casino*.

There is a small visitor center and museum, and there are several reasonably flat well-paved and marked walkways around the site, therefore it is handicap and wheelchair accessible. Parking lot is at GPS 34.611462,-111.839211

Montezuma Well, is approximately 50 miles south of Flagstaff, Arizona off of I-17 at McGuireville, exit 293 on to Bearver Creek Road going east to the entry road at GPS 34.650155,-111.760139. Parking lot is at GPS 34.648726,-111.754433

> *" Hohokam and the Sinagua Indians, to water their crops, used the water from the well and old irrigation ditches that can still be detected in the area. There is a **Hohokam pithouse** and some remains of the **Sinaguan .....**"*

Tuzigoot National Monument, Location: 48 miles southwest of Flagstaff, off U.S. 89A. GPS 34.770282,-112.026585 There is a small gift store and the ruins are a short walk up the hill to the southwest. View of the valley is terrific; this site is worth seeing.

Walnut Canyon National Monument, Location: Off U.S. 66, Interstate 40, 12 miles east of Flagstaff. GPS 35.172046,-111.509203 Although close to Flagstaff; the canyon itself does present a challenge to some as the ruins are in the canyon, and it requires a walk that can be strenuous to some.

Wupatki National Monument, Location: Off U.S. 89, 30 miles north of Flagstaff. This is a not too often visited park as it is not well marked or advertised, but it is worth the ride. The monument is in Sunrise Volcano National Park off of US 89, use GPS 35.37243,-111.575456 that starts at US 89 and ends at US 89 at GPS 35.574857,-111.530821. You will be pleased.

Gallop, New Mexico
Hubbell Trading Post National Historic Site, Location: On Navajo' Indian Reservation, one mile west of Ganado, and 55 miles from Gallup. N. Mexico off of US 191 at GPS 35.710119,-109.552719.

On the road over to the Hubbell Trading post you will pass *Window Rock* at GPS 35.663398,-109.054499; this is where the *Navajo Code Breakers Monument* is; and there is a motel and restaurant there as well as a Navajo Zoo and Library (check for days and hours). The rooms at the motel are interesting and the food at the restaurant is good. Cows outside your door, but.......

Note the Monument and Window Rock Park *with Kiva* is at GPS 35.680716,-109.049644.

Canyon de Chelly National Monument, Location: From Gallup, N. Mex., northwest on U.S. 666 to N. Mex. 264 to U.S. 191 to Chinle and then to the park at GPS 36.152898,-109.539227. Do the South Rim Drive first, then the North Rim Drive, if you still have time. Make sure you stop at the Park Headquarters for refreshments, a peek at what you will see, and a park map. Most of the viewpoint areas are walkable; but some are not or may be difficult for those with impairments.

Phoenix, Arizona

Casa Grande ruins National Monument, Location: Within the town of Coolidge, on Highway 87, halfway between Phoenix and Tucson at GPS 32.995275,-111.536207. The turnoff from Highway 87/287 is at GPS 32.9955,-111.523987. If coming south on I-10, use Exit 190 off of I-10 at GPS 32.938314,-111.70126 and go east on W. McCartney Road to N. Signal Peak Road, then left on W. Randolph Road to a left on Route 87/287

If coming from the south on I-10, take Exit 211 at GPS 32.723465,-111.51595 and go north on Route 87/287.

The interesting part about these ruins is that the park service built a stand-alone roof over the top of the mud adobe buildings to protect each, including the visitors from sun, rain, and whatever. Vultures?

Tonto National Monument, Location: From Phoenix, take U.S. 60-70 to Apache Junction, take State Route 88 at GPS 33.414866,-111.550101 northeast to past the Roosevelt Dam to a right onto Roosevelt Work Center Road (AZ 188 - Apache Road) at GPS

33.672622,-111.15293, then from Roosevelt Work Center Rd, Tonto National Forest, Tonto National Monument, Roosevelt, AZ 85545 turn right at GPS 33.654263,-111.105595 onto the entry road to the Tonto Upper Cliff Dwelling Trail, Tonto National Forest, Tonto National Monument, Roosevelt, AZ 85545 at GPS 33.644697,-111.112761

Santa Fe, New Mexico

Bandelier National Monument, 15 Entrance Road, Bandelier National Monument, Los Alamos, NM 87544 near the top of the mountain by ***Los Alamos National Laboratory*** where the ***Atomic Bomb*** was developed (***Los Alamos Museum*** closed on certain days and hours).

Park is located at GPS 35.778767,-106.270334; you are required to park in the lot, enter the ticket and museum building, and then walk the tour. Most of the walk is reasonably flat, but for those that wish, there is a mountain path to the right that takes you up to the *Cave Houses on the Cliffs*. Wooden ladders are provided for those that want to enter a Cave House. The remainder of the trail snakes down through the woods past a stream and back to your car. Food, drink, and gifts are available there.

Pecos National Historic Park, Location: 25 miles southeast of Santa Fe, via Interstate 25. New Mexico Rt 63, Pecos National Historic Park, Pecos National Historical Park, Pecos, NM 87552 GPS 35.539163,-105.683579

Mancos, Colorado

Mesa Verde National Park, State Highway 10 & U.S. 160, Mancos, CO 81328
The entry road is at GPS 37.340223,-108.411734 and it is a ride on a very twisting road up a mountain and down the other side. Be patient, you will get there, and you will be thrilled that you took the day to drive from ***Monticello, Utah*** where you are staying for a few days so you can visit ***Canyonlands (Newspaper rock), Arches, and National Bridges National parks***.

The *South Road into Canyonlands* is Scenic 211 that starts off of US 191 at GPS 38.074244,-109.350271 and goes through a valley to a large rock that has potholes and aquatic life living on it; and overlooks the river basin on the western side at road's end GPS 38.178215,-109.816927. For some reason, it is named, *Pothole Rock*, gee... Native American *Newspaper rock* is on the road on the way in to the right.

Arches National Park is north of Moab, Utah at GPS 38.611019,-109.607999. Careful, it is easy to miss; it is to the right going north on US 191 and just before the spot where the earth folds under the plates. The road will widen and there will be a right turn arrow, the entry sign is on a rock display set back several feet from the highway on the entry road, thus very difficult to see from US 191 at 60 MPH. The park entry buildings are up the side road, and after entry you will go up the side of the mountain on a winding road, make sure your co-pilot has the camera ready.

Manitou Springs, Colorado
Manitou Cliff Dwellings
10 Cliff Rd, Manitou Springs, CO 80829
38.862810, -104.912996

Appendix III – Current Future of Native America:

This section is a section that has been AI (Artificial Intelligence) generated by Goggle's ™ BARD AI ™system. The author experimented with the AI to see what kind of answers it would produce when asked questions of current relevance. Here are the answers produced.

Q) ... What in 2023 is the current southwestern Native American situation for housing, jobs, healthcare, and economic development?

A) ... The current southwestern Native American situation for housing, jobs, healthcare, and economic development is a complex one. There are many challenges that Native Americans face in these areas, but there are also many successes.

Housing

One of the biggest challenges facing Native Americans is housing. According to the US Department of Housing and Urban Development (HUD), the Native American homeownership rate is only 56%, which is significantly lower than the national average of 65%. This is due to a number of factors, including poverty, lack of access to credit, and discrimination.

The housing crisis on many reservations is still severe, and many Native Americans lack access to quality healthcare. In addition, Native American communities are often struggling to develop their economies and create jobs.

Jobs:

The unemployment rate for Native Americans in the Southwest is still above the national average. According to the U.S. Bureau of Labor Statistics, the unemployment rate for Native Americans in the Southwest was 8.7% in 2022, compared to the national unemployment rate of 3.9%. This is due to a number of factors, including the lack of job opportunities on reservations, the high cost of living, and the lack of education and training among many Native Americans.

There are a number of programs and initiatives that are working to improve job opportunities for Native Americans. The US Department of Labor provides funding for job training programs on tribal lands, and there are a number of non-profit organizations that work to provide job placement services to Native Americans.

Healthcare:
Native Americans in the Southwest face significant challenges accessing quality healthcare.

The healthcare situation for Native Americans in the Southwest is also a challenge. According to the U.S. Department of Health and Human Services, the Native American population has higher rates of chronic diseases such as diabetes, heart disease, and cancer than the general population. Native Americans also have higher rates of infant mortality and suicide than the general population.

There are a number of factors that contribute to the poor health of Native Americans in the Southwest. One factor is the lack of access to healthcare. Many Native Americans live in remote areas where it is difficult to access healthcare. Another factor is the lack of health insurance. Many Native Americans do not have health insurance, which makes it difficult for them to afford healthcare. They are more likely to delay or forgo needed medical care.

Economic Development
The economic development situation for Native Americans in the Southwest is also a challenge. The poverty rate for Native Americans in the Southwest is 26.2%, which is significantly higher than the national poverty rate of 12.3%. The lack of economic development on many reservations is a major factor in the high poverty rate for Native Americans in the region.

There are a number of factors that contribute to the lack of economic development on many reservations. One factor is the lack of infrastructure. Many reservations lack the roads, bridges, and other infrastructure that are needed to attract businesses and create jobs. Another factor is the lack of education and training. Many Native Americans on reservations lack the skills and education that are needed to compete for jobs in the modern economy.

Q) ... What are the southwestern Native Americans doing to help themselves to a better life?

A) … Southwestern Native Americans are working to help themselves to a better life in a number of ways. Some of the things they are doing include:

Improving education and training.
Southwestern Native Americans are working to improve their education and training so that they can compete for jobs in the modern economy. This includes things like starting their own businesses, getting involved in vocational training programs, and attending college.

More and more Native Americans in the Southwest are going to college. In fact, the college enrollment rate for Native Americans in the Southwest is now higher than the national average. This is helping Native Americans to get the skills and education they need to get good jobs and improve their lives.

They are starting their own businesses.
Native Americans are starting businesses in a variety of industries, such as tourism, agriculture, and manufacturing. This is helping to create jobs and economic development on reservations.

In fact, the number of Native American-owned businesses in the Southwest has grown by more than 50% in the past decade. These businesses are creating jobs, generating income, and helping to revitalize Native communities.

Promoting economic development.
Southwestern Native Americans are working to promote economic development on their reservations. This includes things like starting

businesses, attracting new businesses to the reservation, and investing in infrastructure.

Getting involved in politics.
Native Americans in the Southwest are getting involved in politics at a higher rate than ever before. In fact, there are now more Native American elected officials in the Southwest than ever before. This is helping Native Americans to have a voice in government and to advocate for the issues that are important to them.

Improving access to healthcare.
Southwestern Native Americans are working to improve access to healthcare on their reservations. This includes things like building new healthcare facilities, hiring more healthcare providers, and providing transportation to and from healthcare appointments.

They are working to improve their health.
Native Americans are working to improve their health by exercising, eating healthy foods, and getting regular medical checkups. This is helping to reduce the rates of chronic diseases and improve the overall health of the Native American population.

Protecting their culture and traditions.
Southwestern Native Americans are working to protect their culture and traditions. This includes things like teaching their children about their culture, preserving their languages, and participating in traditional ceremonies.

They are preserving their culture and traditions.
Native Americans are working to preserve their culture and traditions through language immersion programs, cultural festivals, and other events. This is helping to keep their culture alive and thriving.

Q) … There are many different types of companies that Southwestern Native Americans could start that would increase their tribal income and stature?

A) … Here are a few ideas:

Tourism businesses. *(This was the # 1 answer)*
The Southwest is a beautiful and culturally rich region, and there is a growing demand for tourism to the area. Southwestern Native Americans could start businesses that cater to tourists, such as hotels, restaurants, and tour companies.

The Southwest is a beautiful and diverse region with a rich history and culture.

Native Americans could start tourism companies that offer tours of their reservations, cultural events, and other attractions. This would help to attract visitors to the region and generate income for the tribes.

Agriculture:
The Southwest has a long history of agriculture, and Native American farmers and ranchers could play a major role in feeding the region and the nation. Native American businesses could start farms, ranches, and food processing companies to produce and distribute food products.

Energy:
The Southwest is home to a significant amount of renewable energy resources, such as solar and wind power. Native American businesses could start companies that develop, generate, and distribute renewable energy to the region and the nation. Manufacturing: The Southwest has a strong manufacturing base, and Native American businesses could start companies that produce a variety of goods, such as electronics, medical devices, and construction materials.

The Southwest is a prime location for renewable energy projects, such as solar and wind power. Starting businesses that are involved in renewable energy would help to create jobs and generate income for the tribes.

Natural resource businesses.

104

The Southwest is home to a variety of natural resources, such as oil, gas, timber, and water. Southwestern Native Americans could start businesses that extract and sell these resources.

Manufacturing businesses.
The Southwest has a number of advantages for manufacturing, such as a low cost of labor and access to natural resources. Southwestern Native Americans could start businesses that manufacture goods, such as food, clothing, and electronics.

Technology businesses.
The Southwest is home to a number of universities and research institutions, which makes it a good place to start technology businesses. Southwestern Native Americans could start businesses that develop and sell new technologies, such as software, medical devices, and renewable energy technologies.

The Southwest is a hub for technology innovation, and Native American businesses could start companies that develop and market new technologies

Businesses that provide services to other businesses.
Native Americans could start businesses that provide services to other businesses, such as accounting, marketing, and consulting. This would help to create jobs on the reservations and generate income for the tribes.

Arts and crafts businesses.
Southwestern Native Americans have a rich tradition of art and crafts. They could start businesses that sell their art and crafts to tourists and other customers.

Starting businesses that sell these products would help to promote Native culture and generate income for the tribes.

Q) … What is the US Government doing to help Native Americans?

A) … There are a number of programs and initiatives that are working to improve housing conditions for Native Americans. The US Department of Housing and Urban Development provides funding for housing programs on tribal lands, and there are a number of non-profit organizations that work to provide housing assistance to Native Americans.

There are a number of factors that contribute to the housing crisis for Native Americans in the Southwest. One factor is the lack of affordable housing on many reservations. The federal government has a trust responsibility to provide housing for Native Americans, but the government has not been able to keep up with the demand. As a result, there is a shortage of affordable housing on many reservations, which drives up rents and makes it difficult for Native Americans to afford to buy a home.

Another factor that contributes to the housing crisis for Native Americans in the Southwest is the high cost of living. The cost of living in the Southwest is generally higher than the national average, which makes it more difficult for Native Americans to afford housing.

There are a number of programs and initiatives that are working to improve job opportunities for Native Americans. The US Department of Labor provides funding for job training programs on tribal lands, and there are a number of non-profit organizations that work to provide job placement services to Native Americans.

There are a number of programs and initiatives that are working to improve healthcare access for Native Americans. The Indian Health Service provides healthcare services to Native Americans on and off reservations, and there are a number of non-profit organizations that work to provide healthcare services to Native Americans.

There are a number of programs and initiatives that are working to improve economic development on reservations. The US Department of Commerce provides funding for economic development projects on tribal lands, and there are a number of non-profit organizations that work to promote economic development on reservations.

Index:

Author:

In the 1940s the author came into being and his parents lived on a farm in the mountains near the Hudson Valley. There was no television, only limited radio and that was the beginning of his misunderstanding of Native America. We had the Lone Ranger, the Cisco Kid, Tales of the Texas Rangers, Gene Autry, and others. These were replaced in the 1950s by the likes of Death Valley Days and Gunsmoke.

As kids we used sticks and stones for bows, arrows, and guns and we used the juice from black walnut husk and red and blue berries to color our faces as we pretended to be 'Indians'.

It wasn't until decades later that I got to the American West and Southwest and started to realize that the 'Indians' were NOT the bad guys, that we the British, the French, the Spanish, and the 'Americans' were the invaders of their lands; that we destroyed their cultures, their food, water, and clothing supplies, and then herded them up like cattle and put them in reservations that were not much better than prisons. Thousands died at our hands; and many were stripped of their language and cultures.

I currently live within throwing distance of two Native American reservations in Arizona, and I have met many of the natives, enjoyed eating their food with them, going to their Powwows and other ceremonies, dancing with them, and learning as much as I can about their history, culture, and lives.

This touring manual is an accumulation and summary of many of my dozens of tours to and into their lands. I hope you enjoyed the text and that you too get to visit and appreciate these people that were and are so brave, ingenious, and intelligent.

Cover:

Wounded Knee 2009 053.JPG

This cover was chosen due to its emotional value, the happenings at Wounded Knee just should never have happened, and the sad part of it is that the destruction and killing happened twice in two different generations.

December 29, 1890
February 27 – May 8, 1973